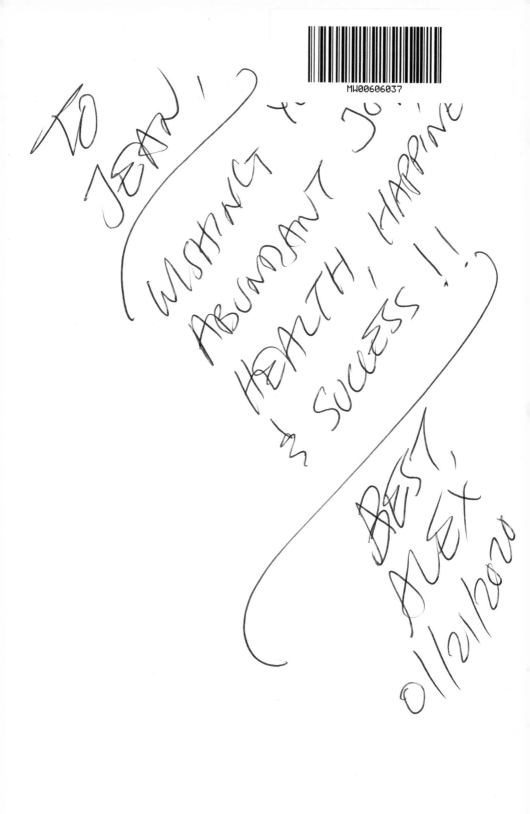

To Jean,

Wishing you abundant joy,
health, happiness,
& success!!

Best,
Alex
01/21/2020

the VOICE WITHIN

An Amazing Journey & To the Depths of Your Soul

ALEX ABOSSEIN

ISBN 978-1-54398-231-2 (hard cover)
ISBN 978--154398-232-9 (eBook)

Special thanks to the following individuals for their active roles in publishing this book:

SARAH IRANI for her artistry in graphics design for the front cover.

JEN DELAGO PEREZ for her assistance in facilitating different tasks related to the production of the book.

REBECCA SHIVEL-GOEBEL, DOUG GOEBEL, DEBORAH WOLF AND MARCIO PACHECO, for the generosity of their time and willingness for their early preview of the book and their comments.

BOOKBABY and all the team members for their editing and publishing efforts.

JOHN LUZZI AND BLASTCAP STUDIOS for making the Audiobook version of this book possible.

C O N T E N T S

Preface xi

Introduction 1

Chapter One - The Age of Innocence 7

Chapter Two - Fear: My Best Friend and Teacher 21

Chapter Three - The Trinity of Self...31

Chapter Four - The Lights Within, Struggle with Self............................47

Chapter Five - Love and Hate Are Self-Generated 63

Chapter Six - You Are the Cause, Not the Effect 73

Chapter Seven - Silence, Knowledge, Fear, Doubt, and at Last, Freedom.............93

    The Castle of Silence 96

    The Castle of Knowledge..97

    The Castle of Will and Daring 99

Chapter Eight - Faith the Shining Armor, Peace the Shield and Sword.............. 107

Chapter Nine - Bliss, I Can Hear Clearly Now! 119

Chapter Ten - The Voices Within 131

    As I Lay Me Down to Sleep 131

    Awakened from Being "Awake" 133

    Can You Love a Monster? 135

    Deception of Addiction and Solution..137

    Determination to Succeed! 139

    Freedom from Emotional Hostage 141

    Freedom from Passive-Aggressive Behavior 143

    Habitual Thinking—Why Excuses? 144

    How to Break the Chain of the Past..145

    Is It Yellow or Gold?...148

    Kindness...150

    Me, Myself, and I..151

    Ordinary or Extraordinary? 153

    Science, Health, and Miracles..155

Solution or Problem? 157

The Anatomy of a Lie 159

The Art of De-memorizing 161

The Attitude of "What Is Wrong" 163

The Cookie Thief 164

The Illusion of Our Perception 166

The Love or the Loveless? 168

The Gift of "Broken"! 170

The Hierarchy of EGO! 172

The Message to Garcia 174

The Mystery of "Self-Esteem"! 176

The Paradigm Shift 178

"The Path to Effectiveness"! 180

The Power of Breath 182

The Power of Expectation 184

The Promise of Future 186

"The Quality Of Our Belief!" 187

The Question of "Good Enough" 189

The Science Behind Reaching Your Desired Goals 191

The Silent Voice Within 191

The Vibration of a Statue 193

The Victim Mentality 195

Time 196

"To Look Forward"! 198

War or a Cup of Tea? 199

What Happens When 2+2=7? 201

What If You Are Having a Bad Day? 203

Why Do We Experience Dis-ease? 205

Will Your Nose Grow If You Lie? 206

Your Attitude: Win-Lose, Win-Win, Lose-Win, Lose-Lose 207

Your Valentine 209

Afterward 211

TO MY MOM AND DAD and my sisters, SUSAN AND LADAN, who showed me from the beginning how beautiful and loving the world is regardless of what may be happening outside, and who have always watched over me.

TO MY WIFE TAMMY, who was the first one with who I shared my voice within. I was energized by her encouragement at each step from conception, and her unconditional love and support has been indescribable.

TO MY AYDEN, who was born to allow me to tap into his unpolluted wisdom and to enjoy sharing this experience together, which is beyond description through any language.

TO ALL MY IN-LAWS, EXTENDED FAMILY, FRIENDS, AND COLLEAGUES who have provided their unconditional support to help me grow. They are the wind under my wings and a joy to interact with.

TO MY DESTINY AND KODA, who sat at my feet with patience for many hours when I was writing.

PREFACE

You cannot go *within* when standing *without*.

Something amazing is about to shift within you as you read this book.

It is not because I have any more knowledge nor any more information than you already have. It is because I have dared to ask your questions aloud and have formulated your answers. Our questions are the same since we are all a drop from the same ocean heading back to the ocean.

Have you ever looked into someone's eyes who is looking back at you with total unconditional love?

It melts your heart and immobilizes you with a magnetic force that you cannot let go.

It is that shift and transformation within that shows you the ocean, inviting you home.

Welcome to looking into my eyes through this book, inviting you to come home!

INTRODUCTION

There was this man who loved mountain climbing. During one of his climbs he fell and broke his back, becoming paralyzed from the waist down. He said that when he was in the hospital, he spent his time by planning how he could climb again. After three years of training and exhaustive inventions, he came up with a hand-driven tractor that helped him climb up mountains. He finally succeeded and, when faced with the reporters at the bottom of the mountain asking him why he did this, he simply said, "Because I can . . . because I can!"

Wouldn't you want to unfold your full capabilities? To move all the barriers you have built by your own thoughts to prove to yourself that you are incapable? What about all those times you debated back and forth, wanting to do something, but that hidden voice kept you back. Don't you ever wonder about that ageless being inside you that watches everything you do and at times comforts you, embraces you, cherishes you, and praises you when you are doing good things, and at other times looks away not, wanting to witness the pain and suffering that you bring to yourself by doing wrong. But is it looking away or helplessly watching the scars formed within your soul, hoping that you will see the sorrow in its eyes leading to change your path to a direction that will guide you out of this endless circle?

Where does everything begin and end? What is that beginning that we call God? Is he a bearded old man with love and compassion flowing from his eyes? Is he that hidden voice inside each of us that makes us to go forward when we don't even know why? What is the purpose behind happiness, pain, sorrow, love, and hate? What is it that we are here to do? The time will come for each of us to question our faith, to face our faith, to test our faith, to cherish or to hate it, to curse our faith or to love it for providing the choice to make decisions, the right ones or the wrong ones. But is there right or wrong, or is it all part of our growth? How do you define righteousness if there is no sin; how do you define goodness if there is no evil; and how could you do more of the right thing if you do not know of the bad?

It is said that we shall not enter Heaven unless we become like children again.

Aren't you curious to find out what this is all about? To be born free from all thoughts, to live carrying and forming ourselves to what we believe the way of life is, and to become like children again to have eternal peace. Does it make sense? Isn't there a lot of why, what, and how in all of this?

There are so many "whys" and "whats" that make your head spin, but you have to make it spin if you want it to move. There are no shortcuts. There is no way out other than searching for it. For whatever reason, each of us has to find that on our own. You cannot pay for it; you cannot have someone find it and give it to you. You, with all guards down, all barriers destroyed, and with total surrender are the only one who can experience it. Once experienced, it can be cherished, loved, and accepted because the struggle is over; you're home at last.

How could you live with these questions and not be angry? Angry for not knowing why you do the things you do. The lucky ones are the ones who do not question it. Somehow in the cosmic laws of the universe, it is agreed that this temporary relief of playing ignorant is only a short childish game, it is a mirage, it is a dream that will last for a short while until you decide it is time to face the truth. When you review the decisions, actions, and goals of your life, you realize that all stemmed from this basic question—"Who am I?" Who am I when I am not doing anything, when I am not going anywhere, when I am not acting to please anyone? And it is just me with no thought or activity? Do I like it or is the prospect of having no thought so scary that I need to hide behind some type of activity or be occupied with someone else's interactions to forget about myself, and maybe the pain of wanting to find myself will go away? Indeed, it will be hidden for a while in the abyss of your soul, crying out to be found. One day you have to let it free, when you're tired of holding it back and ignoring its existence. To ignore its existence is to ignore yourself, and you do exist. The perception of who you are to acknowledge your existence may come from a different angle than the universal point of view, but you're not a mirage or fantasy; you and the experiences that form you do exist. You must feel pain and sorrow, you must embrace happiness and love, same as sadness and hate, until you realize that it is not positive or negative, it is not evil or angelic. It exists to serve a purpose.

External sources define who we are by giving us the inputs that we like or dislike. Very quickly our definition of who we are is formed by what we think everyone else wants us to be. Once you believe this, the form is set, and it will take many years of pain and sorrow to break this cast and rebuild it based on what really is, which will be the true definition of who one is. To live with the assumption that your actions have no consequences, as opposed to believing that what we do in life will echo through eternity, creates a complete set of different goals and lifestyles.

If your definition of who you are is based on a religious belief that says earthly things are for a short while and eternal life awaits us in paradise, then the stage is set, the lights are on, and the audience is ready to cheer for your acting. Your approach to every decision of your life is from that angle. To love and to hate is based on the basic belief that punishment or reward is awaiting you in another world. Fear grows larger and larger. What if what I am doing is not good enough to secure my happiness in eternal life, and how long is eternity? Do I get a second chance? How sad it is to be a certain way just because you are afraid of the alternative. They say human nature is sinful. Does it not bother you to question this, to wonder what we have done that is so terrible we have been condemned to a sinful life, that we have to fight for our freedom? And what is it about freedom that it has to be just the right amount? Too little of it makes you fight for more with all your powers, and too much of it makes you give it up, so you stop feeling out of control.

What if your definition of who you are is whatever makes you feel good and satisfies you physically? The purpose of life is to enjoy your body and your physical experiences to their maximum. That makes sense, doesn't it? The world is limited to what we can see, to whatever your five senses can feel exists, right? If it is pleasing to the eyes, I want it. If it smells good, I must have it. If it sounds nice, I would like to possess it so I can use it at my discretion, and the list goes on. Sounds interesting, but what makes something pleasing to the eyes or to have a pleasant smell, or what are the ingredients that make something acceptable or unacceptable to our senses? Doesn't it come from an unseen source? How do you explain the brain activity that sets the criteria for your likes and dislikes? It can't be sensed by any of our sensory feelings. It is not documented in any place of the body that can be opened and read. The criterions are formed from all our experiences as we age, with options to change, disregard, modify, and reevaluate at our will. But only you possess the knowledge of what is stored inside you. It is like entering a castle with a lot of rooms, and you never know what it is behind each door. Each of us holds the key to the door, to our lifetime experiences and thoughts within. Then, how could life's purpose be limited to our feelings when the very source that initiates those feelings cannot be felt or seen? Isn't it safe to say that if your purpose in life is based on physical pleasures only, then it cannot be complete, and other aspects are needed to complete the picture?

What if the only way to find out who you are is to spend time in solitary, to find yourself without any contact with the outside world? How can you find yourself when your experiences are limited only to yourself? How can the player and the coach be the same? Our interactions with others, our observation of others' behaviors toward each other and their rejections, acceptance, love, hate, beauty, and ugliness as defined by different people, will coach us to the right path.

What if your definition of who you are is to live mindlessly, accepting everything as it is without questioning the beginning or the end or the process? This is just the way it has always been; therefore, it must be the right way and the only way. This is the calmness before the storm. It will not be long before your definition of life, to be preoccupied with physical attachments or personal attachments, will be completed, and you will find yourself empty, looking for another fix. Looking for something else to attach to, something to give meaning to your existence—another spouse, another child, another house, another job. Before you know it, this cycle of life ends with an emptiness that makes your soul cry for your attention, calling you home, hoping that in another life you may listen to its cry sooner.

To embrace is to love, and to let go is to love more. Knowing that the desire to hold is to possess, and to possess is to rule, and to rule is to be separated, and separation is to be apart from ourselves, and to part from ourselves is to be independent from the divine force that created us, or to be alone in an endless universe that can only be described as hell as we know it.

Too many questions, too many unknowns, too many "ifs" and "hows" and "whys." Why can't we just live? What in the mechanics of creation makes us search for these assumptions and theories without the assurance of their accuracy and their truth? It has been said that the secret of the universe will be revealed to you when you die. To live not knowing why—guessing, struggling, and searching to find what will be given to you when you die—is a never-ending story. But again, maybe that is what our form of life is supposed to be: a never-ending story, a childish game to entertain. Somehow, it is hard to believe that all the pain, sorrow, happiness, love, and hate is just a game. But indeed, it may be a childish game of hide and seek, and once you're tired of hiding all your life, the desire to be found will spring up from the roots of your being. It is comforting to know that there are a lot of consistencies in life and, if you are patient and observant enough to find the links, they will be revealed. That is the best news ever; if this is true, then from what we know, we'll be able to find the unknowns that we are searching for. We have done it successfully for centuries; we predict based on assumptions, and the right answers follow. If this can be done to travel to other physical planets, why can't it be done to find a path to travel within the depth of our soul, guiding it home?

At last, after all the confusion, there is hope of finding ourselves. Hope, my good old friend, my companion, my teacher, the voice inside echoed by cheering, unknown, divine faces within my soul. Hope, my cane that I have leaned on through all my struggles, let me embrace you and never let go. It is good to see you again.

CHAPTER ONE

THE AGE OF INNOCENCE

Is it possible to know a book by reading only one chapter? Is it possible to explain the reasons behind all our experiences within the time frame of one life span? There are too many injustices and confusions to describe in one lifetime. How could you explain the poor, the rich, the healthy, the sick, the ruler, the beggar, the abuser, and the abused's pain, sorrow, and happiness, as they unfold only in one lifetime? Is it justice for one to be healthy, happy, and content when the other is sick, poor, and miserable? Of course not; justice as we know it claims equality for all human beings.

We enter this world with no agenda, with a blank canvas ready to be painted on with the most beautiful painting of our lives as we gather our experiences, and yet the painting may turn out to be the most frightening picture ever. How can we ensure the beauty of this piece of art called *The Story of My Life*? You are the artist; the images, the story, the scenery, the beauty and ugliness stem from your thoughts, becoming reality. Still, we choose to question and wonder why it is not what we had expected it to be when it is time to put down the last stroke and watch the painting unfold as we remember the events and emotions behind each stroke.

The age of innocence, the birth of an angel, the freedom of an eagle, the playfulness of a tiger cub transforms to guilt, hate, dissatisfaction, loss of purpose, and boredom over the years as we grow older. Somehow the game gets old, and since our perception of "old" is to die and the natural tendency of body is to live, a conflict arises within ourselves.

The fear grows larger and larger. I do not want to jump but I have no choice; my creation is designed to make me walk forward toward the edge of the cliff. I have not seen the valley below, but I know that it is at the end of my path. It is where everyone else disappears to. The ones I loved forever, the ones I loved less, the ones I knew, and the ones that I did not want to know; they all eventually left me behind as I know I will one day too.

But once I am at the end of my road and looking back for a last glance at the long path I have traveled, how can I ensure that I'll be happy to say I enjoyed the trip? Indeed, I learned a lot, loved a lot, cried when I had to, and laughed even when I did not want to; but just because I felt good, played a lot, taught some, fought a little, and felt on top of the world on some occasions, at other times I wanted to stop living because the pain seemed unbearable, carried others on my shoulder, and let others carry me when I had no strength to walk.

The beginning of life starts with very little memory. Time and our experiences shape us to some degree, but it seems like there is much more in making a man's character than his environment. People with identical environments and backgrounds grow up to be totally different, and sometimes they even become the best and the worst of humanity, in total opposition of each other.

The people with all types of upbringings and different lifestyles end up rejecting the forms they were meant to fit into and finally choose their own. Some lose their own identity and become what pleases their parents or someone else they seek acceptance from. It will take decades before they realize that their image of who they are belongs to someone else. Our creation and evolution cannot accept separation within ourselves. In order to be whole as a person, you must be in agreement with all the characters that exist within you, otherwise the pain of separation and internal division forces you to seek that alignment of soul, body, and spirit called "peace."

There is no other way; pain is designed to be your teacher and your divine coach. We tend to listen to it when it becomes unbearable and forget about it once it disappears. Like old companions who know each other's every move, pain is also aware of our stubborn rejection of its signals and knows that it will need to come back with greater intensity if we do not learn from its warnings. It will take a long time before emotional sufferings start showing up as physical pains, but its complications and presence in one form or the other is undeniable.

One way or another, we each have to find our path regardless of paying attention or disregarding the guiding signals along the way. The pleasure of doing it my wrong way, rather than listening to the warnings of others, is indescribable. Of course, we know that the definition of wrong may simply be something different than what has been accepted as standard practice by society. The arrogance of not listening to others is needed to form our individuality, but yet we all learn from each other's experiences to find our personal paths. This combination of "show me the way" and "I have the desire to find it myself" is like teaching obedience to a wild and free animal. Indeed, we will all find our path guiding us home, and yet each one is parallel to the others but not the same. It cannot be the same; we are all individuals with the blessings to choose and make decisions regardless of how controlling our society may be.

But is having the choice to make our own decisions a blessing or a curse? Isn't it easier to live mindlessly, following the directions and guidelines set by others? Of course not; we all look at a beautiful race horse and confirm that his usage as a farm animal does not fit—there is something missing. The horse seems like he was created to do something else, to run freely with all his powers. It is the same for humans; living a robotic lifestyle does not fit. There is something missing. The beauty of creating something that none else has ever made, the excitement and pleasure of forming yourself as an individual with no duplication possibilities, is just what was intended and cannot be denied. Its denial is to deny the very nature of your existence, and experience has shown that shortly, the pain of denying yourself turns to depression, dissatisfaction, boredom, anger, hatred of yourself and then others, and is eventually reflected as pain and illness of the physical body.

But why do we conform ourselves to shapes that are unsatisfactory and inconsistent with what we really want? Can't we simply wish to be a certain way, be that, and be happy with receiving what we asked for? Sounds very simple, but it's the most complex wish we have ever known. Time is the variable that impacts our wish. What we ask for today in total happiness and content is not so tomorrow. Is it simply passing time creating dissatisfaction of what we had asked for, or the desire to constantly search, worry, and wonder that not having goals will be the end of our experiences, and not having experiences equate to our death—the finishing line, the mystery of all times, the unknown.

Not wanting to face the unknown keeps us searching for more and more as we grow older and older. The childish games, the thrills, the occasions, the parties, the gatherings, the possessions, the prestige—they all become old. The increasing heartbeat of a thrill, the anxiety of a short romantic glance into someone else's eyes, the excitement of meeting an old friend—they all become just another thing that needs to be done. It seems as the artist and the audience change positions as the movie of life gets closer toward the end. The excitement of being in the midst of all actions changes to simply observing of our own actions as they unfold in a routine way in front of our eyes.

How can it be? What in the cosmic wisdom of the universe makes it so? It seems that creation of every action, every live being, every idea starts with some form of foreplay and ends with some glorious climax. There is always something at the end that makes the trip worthwhile.

Then how can the end of our lives be the end of our experiences? On the contrary, it is the climax that we have been waiting for all our lives, to create the afterlife that we want. It's not an end but a beginning. A time to celebrate, a time to cherish and evolve into another phase of our journey. To find love within ourselves, to find salvation within ourselves, to find peace within ourselves, and yes, at last, to find the divine within ourselves when all the prerequisites are met and we are ready to be borne into divine beings that we were meant to fit into.

Oh, at last, thank you for showing me the dim light at the end of the tunnel. Now I can see in the darkness that surrounds me with all different ideas, all different philosophies, all different religions, and all assumptions that there is a direction of hope to find you. You know, it is not as confusing as I thought it was before. Especially with all these ideas about how to find you, and yet you are so close. All my life I looked for you in the skies, beyond the sun, beyond the moon, in the other planets and in the stars, and yet I now feel your presence within me; you're closer than my breath. I wish I could see you now; I want to look into your eyes and find the answers to my many questions. I want to know the reason for my existence, the reason for my pains and happiness. I want to know your reasoning for other's sufferings and pains. I want to tell you all the things that I refuse to see and hear for my heart overflows with sorrow. Grant me this one wish and let me taste the truth from the cosmic points of view, and maybe the pain of my ignorance will be lessened.

No, no, that cannot be your voice. It does not make sense, even me with my small limited knowledge of your wisdom cannot believe that my happiness and sadness are only measured by what the others are experiencing. But you know, something within me tells me to look for the mirage that clouds the truth, and yes, I can see it now.

But how do we enter into this vicious cycle of measuring our happiness by other's miseries? When others fail, we feel sorry for their loss and failure, and then suddenly a small note of a thought dangling in the back of our mind plays a familiar tone. It becomes more and more harmonious and profound, giving us the assurance and pleasure of feeling better about ourselves, since our situation is better than that of the person who has experienced failure. Amazingly, we feel better about ourselves when others' lives are in more chaos than ours. The guilt is just a natural byproduct of hopelessly witnessing others suffocating and experiencing pain, but that it assures us we're in a better position than others cannot be denied. It reminds us to thank our blessings for our position in life and to move forward.

So, if measuring our position in life against others is not the answer, then what is? Haven't we all learned that everything is relative? All our likes and dislikes, all our education, all our competitions, all our business lives, all our trainings and upbringings teach us that you win, you succeed, you are promoted, and yes, you survive based on how you can be better than others. How can it be that all we know and train at all times is related and measured by comparing ourselves to others, but once we get to the quest for the meaning of life and finding the very root of our being, we are expected to stop and giving it all up? How can we constantly train ourselves to be so strong while our weaknesses are the keys to finding our true essence?

Confusing, isn't it? All the evidence points to the even more confusing truth. It is almost as if there is a huge cosmic conspiracy to stop us from finding the meaning of life, the meaning of our existence. But again, do you value something that was given to you without any effort? Does something that is handed to you without you wanting it hold the same value as something that you struggled to gain with all your power? When you search and search, fight all the crusades, feel the thirst of wanting to know, and live in the pain of separation and your ignorance, it leads to a small sign of hope that gives you the strength to continue; then that is the time when the value of what you are hoping to find is established, and it is directly proportional to the time, effort, strength, and persistence that was put into finding it. To reach for something after all the battles are won deserves receiving the grand prize and holding it close to your heart for all time. Gold itself is not demandable; it is the attention of all the people looking for it that makes it scarce, makes it valuable, makes it desirable.

It is amazing, and faith promises that it is true, for the love inside is the only thing that can be taken with us. The hate inside will accompany us back and back again until we recognize its emptiness and find its antidote. The forgiveness is what will set us free, not from others but from ourselves. The freedom that is required in order to assure us the love that we were promised as our birthright. Somehow, the birthright that we were given had to be earned during our lifetime. The credit of love that was extended to us at birth had to be cashed out at the end to ensure our clean conscience, the clean record that we were entrusted to be born into. Maybe everything can be summarized by saying that a piece of divine was separated from the force that is called the beginning as we know it to be formed into a small shell. It was entrusted to us to find, expand, explore, discover, teach, guide, and enjoy the beauty of physical forms without shattering the true essence of love, goodness, peace, and happiness that was originated from. The only way to reunite is to be of the same form, of the same energy, of the same essence, otherwise there is no chance of reconciliation. Otherwise, reconciliation must be delayed, awaiting refinement of the spirit back to its original form and hoping that our preoccupation with the different shells that we are born into will not distract us.

Indeed, what child does not ache to reunite with his parents after being away for a while, wanting to run with all his powers and throw himself into their open arms, tell them how much he has missed them, and share everything that he has learned along the way? What parents will not await the reunion, worrying, praying, and hoping that their child will safely return soon? Simply said, the only word justifying the cause of delay for reconciliation can be named hell.

So, where did it all begin, and can we find ourselves by looking at that beginning that started it all? Isn't it true that each of us is the observer of all our experiences looking through a telescope to the end of the universe, or through a microscope to the smallest particles within? Isn't it true that we all see with the "eyes" of the "I" of this inner being that has no physical eyes, but yet at times we have the clarity to see through its eyes from the same angle that the creator views it all?

Let's assume that we take a 747 jet to the junkyard and disassemble it with all the pieces spread throughout. That night there is a big thunder and lightning storm followed by an earthquake. What are the chances that in the morning, somehow the jet is totally assembled, with all its controls and machinery operating with perfect precision? Yes, there was a big bang of cosmic energy change, but the assumption of anything less than an architect bringing it all together is incomprehensible.

Science will never find the creator since science has no heart. That source that created it all can only be found by wholeness and completeness. That wholeness presents itself only when the left and right brain harmonize with each other to operate as one. They say compassion is the byproduct of this marriage.

Each scientist can testify that there is a driver behind the scene. Each scientist can vouch that the silence that exists between two thoughts does something as the driver behind the scene guides us. That silence appears to have no action, but it determines it all by directing us to choose choice A or choice B of the next thought. Each of us finds ourselves with an awareness that is before any feeling and before any thought that cannot be explained.

After all the scientific explorations and what may be qualified as evolvements and all the amazing discoveries, we still have not been able to prove the existence of our core essence, of love. Even scientists fall in love, protect their loved ones, take care of others, and cry when their heart melts with joy or sorrow, but they still have not scientifically proven that love exists.

They can show that brain level activities drop to change for some better outcome, injury heals faster, and immune systems increase when loving conditions and thoughts are experienced, but there is no scientific proof that love exists.

Finding the creator through science requires using the same technology that can explain that love exists. It is so simple but yet forgotten by many who look for it outside, not realizing that the pearl is hidden inside the shell.

My most favorite time with my son was when I used to tuck him in and he could communicate well at the age of two, not yet polluted by the society and barely able to express himself. Our long conversations of what he remembered before he was born, with very little reasons to believe that he had any justification to have gathered that information from his limited physical contacts, resonated deep within me.

Any two-year-old has the ability to prove the existence of creation and love. All that's needed is for the scientist to turn back the clock to when they were two years old, and that forgotten ability will reappear with instrumental perfection that cannot be found in any physical laboratory.

This reminds me of one of my favorite stories; there was a yogi who was dancing by himself in the middle of the street as people watched and ridiculed him for dancing alone. They approached him and questioned, "Why are you dancing alone?" His response: "Who says I am alone!"

Ego dictates that there is nothing but the shell alone, and the pearl inside whispers quietly to have faith, to listen to the quiet voice within, to dare to open the shell to find the pearl inside and see that you are never alone.

So maybe the answer is much simpler than we had thought. Maybe it is nothing other than finding joy in being. Maybe it is as simple as they had said: "Chop wood, carry water before enlightenment, and chop wood, carry water after enlightenment."

A mirage is defined as an optical illusion, hallucination, fantasy, or figment of one's imagination, or something that appears real or possible but is not. Scientists have shown that the brain fires up the same cluster of neurons whether we physically play the piano or sit quietly and play it in our head.

What does that one person who sees the mirage as so real in her own world that she believes it to be real when the rest of the world sees it as a mirage? If she sees water in her own reality, then why can the water not be manifested physically to satisfy that thirst?

Isn't it true that we all see our own reality in our own way, while the rest of the outside world may see it differently?

What link transforms things from what we see inside to what materializes in the physical plane of the outside world called reality?

An explosion in transformation requires a spark, a fuse, and an explosive to create a perfect combustion of conversion. We know that the brain sees, and the eyes are only portal inputs. Transformation requires the inner eyes to see and the inner belief to feel it as it already exists in order for the mirage to become the reality.

Swami Rama tells many stories of instant manifestation in his book, *Living with the Himalayan Masters.* What is the difference between a yogi that says "be" and "it is" and the thirsty desert wonderer who says "be" but the water only appears as a mirage? The answer to all the above may simply be in how we view our being.

When we are joyful in being, we enjoy all prosperity and abundance, promoting it and sharing it. When we are not, we look to gain money and keep it for ourselves, being greedy and protecting it by all means.

————————

When we are joyful in being, we enjoy creation and manifestation at will, as there are no boundaries as we fly through life. When we are not, we see everything as obstacles, borders, restrictions with heaviness at every step.

————————

When we are joyful in being, we see the word "impossible" as "I'm possible." When we are not, we give up, quit, and get exhausted before reaching our goals, as they seem too far away to be possible.

————————

When we are joyful in being, we appreciate this experience at its every step, from when we enter this world and up to when we leave. When we are not, we question our beginning and every step after that, and are terrified of where we will go.

————————

When we are joyful in being, we recognize our power and that we can choose the outcome by what we choose now. When we are not, we are content to be powerless victims of cosmic conspiracy of the mirage of our ego.

————————

When we are joyful in being, we see the unity and connection of all, and celebrate that unification. When we are not, we only see separation and look for unlimited reasons to be offended and to divide more.

When we are joyful in being, we say "be" and the water appears, since it is the same essence as the source of our existence and the energy that allows us to have this experience. When we are not, we say "be" and the water is a mirage, since it can never transform to our reality through a catalyst that is different from its energy.

———————

So, what is our true essence of being, and what causes our misconception and its distortion? Like the images at the bottom of pond that are not exactly where they are physically located when we reach for them, it is that illusion of looking through self-created lenses that begins our confusion.

We come as infants from an energetic world with an absolute knowledge of what our true essence is, and somehow we get derailed for a while as we grow out of being toddlers. We circle back after years of wondering, trying to find our beginning and the freedom that once we had, since the emptiness that we feel cannot be filled by anything else other than that essence which completes us.

Joyfulness, peace, love, compassion, and happiness are considered our optimum goals, and yet we dismiss the teachers who show us how to live it, since they cannot communicate verbally. If the teachers lead by example, then the best prospects would be infants and toddlers. There is no record of any infants or toddlers desperately seeking appointments with psychiatrists and counselors in order to deal with anxiety, depression, and emotional issues in an attempt to feel better and be joyful, simply because they already feel good. There are no statistics of any armies of children attacking other nations and destroying lives. There has never been a toddler who intentionally planned to abolish others in the name of humanity or otherwise. There has been no record of any infant presenting their case in court to sue others and be vicious because of a quarrel. No one has ever heard of an infant or toddler spreading deceitfulness motivated by their personal agenda.

Historically, even when adults have come forward to tell us that the children are the true teachers and have the true essence of our source, we have disregarded them as crazy blasphemers deserving punishment for such ideas. When Jesus was asked by high priests and pharisees, "Who shall enter the kingdom of Heaven?" he responded, "I tell you the truth, you shall not enter the kingdom of Heaven unless you become like children again." In the ignorance of those fixated on their reality, limited to only what they could see, they responded, "This man is crazy; we must become like children again and enter our mothers' wombs in order to get to Heaven." How wrong can we be in the name of ego that promotes "only what I see exists, only if you are like me are you good, only if you have my status are you worthy, and only I can measure how much love may exist."

> *"Learn to get in touch with the innermost essence of your being. This true essence is beyond the ego. It is fearless; it is free; it is immune to criticism: it does not fear any challenge. It is beneath no one, superior to no one, and full of magic, mystery, and enchantment."* — DEEPAK CHOPRA

Who would you be if you were not raised by your parents and others who, in the name of their love, taught you all they knew? Esther Hicks profoundly explains that "it is like being born into a village where everyone is limping and when you start running freely, they scold you that you should not do such a thing and you should be limping like others. Finally, when you do not perform, they club your knees to ensure that your confined happiness is being met when you limp like the rest with limitations."

Beneath the surface of all actions, sits still the quietness of your essence. It is love, it is loving, and it is beyond that. Embrace it and meet yourself again!

CHAPTER TWO

FEAR: MY BEST FRIEND AND TEACHER

As I look out the window, the sound of raindrops on the roof and the sadness of the sky keep me in a trance with old images going through my mind as this question echoes in my thoughts. What are my fears? Not past and not future, but in this moment of peace and tranquility with no one around except me. Oops, I mean almost me. Sorry, old friend, how can I forget about you who has witnessed everything that has happened to me all my life? You are the one who knows all about me, and yes, you are the one who truly knows my fears. I have deceived myself and many, but you are the one who bared the scars of my hiding. You are the one who always told me to stop, it is time, it is time to face them now. I see my reflection in the window and wonder who the old person is looking back at me, but then I see you looking out, ageless as the first time I heard your voice calling out to me, "Don't be afraid. It will be fine. You'll see."

Fear, you have held on to me all my life, and I don't find comfort in you anymore. It is time to say our goodbyes and part. I know, my friend, you have shown me so much that all my life was based on your teachings. All my goals, all my dreams, all my purpose in life was paved by your standards and guidance, but I had thought that you did not exist. What are you whispering? It was my ego shadowing your existence. Ah yes, I agree it was my ego not wanting to accept that I am not brave enough to face you. You see, if I pretend that you don't exist, I can deceive myself into being much happier in my misery.

All my life I had thought that cowardice is to believe in fear, and now I realize that denying you is the true indication of my lack of bravery. True bravery is acknowledging your existence. Pretending that you do not exist and planning all our lives around you is just your mischievous mastery in action, proving our hypocrisy. In order to be brave enough to embrace you, we have to acknowledge you. There is only one way to let you go and "that is to embrace you" with all our being, to thank you for all your teachings, to say farewell, the last goodbye to an old friend and teacher; and yes, we cannot do that to something that we do not believe is real, and you and your experiences are as real as I am.

You have shown many of your faces before with your artistic mastery. It seems like you have a face for every occasion. Hate, deception, jealousy, sadness, war, rudeness, prejudice, and sickness are only a small number of your masks, but what amazes me most is that you were created to protect us from physical harms, and yet you control every aspect of our lives. You build our futures. You make us and form us into the monsters that we despise. The most beautiful sculpture was created at birth, and then you came along and little by little, chipping away piece by piece, changed it to a piece of sharp-edged stone that cannot be touched.

It amazes me to know that most of our decisions are based on and limited by different fears, and that almost all of our fears are illusions created by our own minds. You see, we tend to abuse mother nature each time we interfere with its intent. Simply said, if you are attacked by a lion and the chemical reactions in your brain demand that you run and hide, that is a good display of what the nature really intended. But when the next day you choose not to come out since you may face the lion again—that is the mischievous brain in play.

Tell me your secrets. I promise to only share them with those who are as thirsty as I am.

No need to worry; somehow the knowledge of your existence can only be revealed to those who have been so thirsty for so long that they are willing to drink you despite the horrible taste. Rumi's famous poem echoes in my mind: "I saw Grief drinking a cup of sorrow and called out, 'It tastes sweet, does it not?' 'You've caught me,' Grief answered, 'and you've ruined my business. How can I sell sorrow, when you know it's a blessing?'"

The journey to find your secret is as if the punishment seems too much for the crime. But what crime, what is it that we have done against the master cosmic laws that deserves such punishment? To be confused all our lives and somehow to find our path to the point of exhaustion, realizing that sorrow is a blessing and fear is designed to guide us home. Disregard your physical body and pretend that you have a newborn's brain but are able to walk, travel, and observe your surroundings. Let's take a walk in the most dangerous cities, swim in the wildest oceans, run in the cruelest jungles, and face the most horrifying animals. But wait, how can it be possible? How come I have no fear? Why do I feel no inhibition? I am free at last, as I was in the beginning.

Then, what is it that I have traded for my loss of freedom and indeed innocence, and what are the universal intentions for me doing so? Is it just listening to the voice of fear that has caused me to be this way? If that is so, which voice is it and from where did it originate? Was it incorporated into our being from birth and it is discovered as we age, or is it the creation of our mind based on our physical experiences or imaginations?

It cannot be said any more beautifully than Jana Stanfield's famous words: "If I refuse to listen to the voice of fear, would the voice of courage whisper in my ear?" It is very simple yet very true, and amazingly we all miss it, abuse it, and choose not to recognize that darkness is nothing but the absence of light, courage is nothing but the absence of fear, and fear is nothing but absence of awareness. The awareness to differentiate between healthy fear, which keeps us from dangers, and the unhealthy fear, which keeps us from loving our birthright to enjoy and celebrate our existence.

Now, how do we differentiate between these fears? How can we know which to listen to and which to ignore? Simply said, if you had the choice of listening to two counselors and each had the following credentials, which would you choose? One is strong, wise, quiet, methodical, loving, and observant, and only speaks when it is absolutely necessary for something to be said on your behalf. The other one is jittery, anxious, nervous, and annoying, constantly talking and informing you of all the potential issues that may or may not be in your best interest. The choice is obvious; the first advisor is the best companion on this journey. But most of us choose to listen to the second counselor without realizing the complications, loss of freedom, and other problems this selection will bring us.

The good news is that as human beings, we are predictable and do create and follow certain patterns. Along the same path, we develop relationships with whatever is happening in our lives and become attached to it. By attachment, we create energy that can be enjoyable and loving, or painful and disturbing. But based on our knowledge of the universe, we know that energy cannot be destroyed; it can only change forms. We recognize that the energy created by the false fear can be annoying and unpleasant, and will disturb our peace and happiness. Knowing this truth prompts us to find a way to transfer this energy to something else that can have positive outcomes for us.

There are certain steps that must be followed to accomplish this task. The first step requires courage to face our fears, then the desire and persistence to explore them.

Acceptance of what is found is the next step to healing and converting this energy; and finally, we must take certain actions to respond to it and to change its direction toward what can be peaceful and positive in our lives.

One may say that recognizing and following these steps is beyond a novice's abilities and requires professional interference at all times. Of course, we recognize which counselor is speaking at this time, and in order to ask him to be silent, the following clarifications can be made, knowing that knowledge is the torch that will guide us through the darkness of ignorance and fear.

That formless being inside us that watches all our actions at all times and gives us approval or disapproval will insist on increasing your emotional pains and dissatisfaction with your daily activities to make you develop the courage needed to face your fears. Time is required to make this process as smooth as possible. There are many ingredients needed to develop this, and they will all present themselves at the right times, when you are ready to align yourself with the universal intentions and surrender. All we need is to be aware and sensitive to recognize the signals along the way. One may question our ability to recognize these signals; that can be answered by the simple truth that the pain and discomfort of this misalignment of peace will force you to build the courage required to take the necessary actions. Once you recognize that you are tired of running away, the desire to stop and face the bully will strengthen you to do what is needed to confront your demons.

Now, with courage guiding and carrying you, the strength of turning around and walking toward fear will appear. Easier said than done, and indeed consistent with the voice echoed inside insisting that you are not ready to see your fears, not now and not yet. The reinforcement of your will to confront is needed again.

Obviously, we realize which counselor's voice this is, and by the knowledge of truth we learn to ignore it. However, you must be prepared to face and see the most horrifying pictures of your life as you start traveling back on the path that you always used for running away. By shouting that fear and doubts are nothing but illusions, the dragon that had been chasing you through your life will become smaller and smaller. Soon, by desire and strength for reaching for the reality of your fear, the huge shadow of the monster that had been chasing you away shall reduce to its actual size. The giant that you had been hiding from all your life is just a scarecrow created by your own thoughts, which will vanish once its true identity is recognized.

I can hear the melody of the old tone playing in the background again. The old familiar song of "acceptance," such a simple phrase but so difficult to accept, so difficult to acknowledge. Our nature has conditioned us to go forward without giving up; it is the root of desire to our success and progression. It seems that to accept is contradictory to the origin of our very fuel that ignites our strength to go forward, and rightfully so, since we interpret that as to giving up the battle and surrendering. It is so hard to accept because we equate acceptance with failure, and yet it can be the biggest blessing that man has ever known. Accepting what you cannot change is as important as changing what you cannot accept. Acceptance is nothing but recognizing that there are some things that cannot be changed at this time and at this junction of our lives, and realizing that under the existing circumstances, it is OK to stop for a while in preparation of erasing these scary thoughts from our brains.

At last, the moment of truth that we have been anticipating along the way will come near. The preparation is over and it is time for action. The transition with all its discomforts and pains must be made to reverse this flow of energy, to create the positive outcome that we need in our lives.

Indeed, when the student is ready, the teacher will appear and the lesson is learned. Another word, the seed of the universal knowledge, is constantly thrown and is available, but the transfusion to the final product is only made when the soil has been prepared and is ready to accept its development to its final stage. The preparation of the soil is only possible when the initial three ingredients have been included and followed through with persistence, patience, and perseverance.

Let's explore more of this mysterious maestro, fear. When we are hungry, we eat and we feel better. When we are cold, we find clothing and we feel well again. When it is raining, we find shelter and we are comforted. All the above assist us in recognizing our universal default of joyfulness.

However, our misconception starts after our minimum needs have been satisfied. More food, more shelter, more clothing, more power, more prestige will bring us more joy, so we start planning and strategizing to collect and to hold in search of more happiness and the good feelings once we had.

The progression from following to having more is the anticipation of, "What if we lose it?" That is when the fear begins. Fear is our interpretation of the uncomfortable feeling of a loss of something that we already have, or something that we want to have but cannot get. This can be for any tangible material thing or intangible emotional needs.

Only 1 percent of our fears are real. The other 99 percent of the time, fear depends on how we process the events of our lives. This illusion of our mind disappears when we go toward it, and it gets larger when we run away from it, just like a shadow on the wall.

The best way to avoid fear is to live in the NOW: "The past is history, future is mystery, and NOW is where peace is. That is why it is called present—because it is a gift."

What is it about darkness that frightens us? We pray for daylight and stand guard when the darkness appears. Why is that? And what experiences have caused us to show such universal reactions as human beings? It is the same insecurity that we feel in a dark alley, the same fear that stops us from entering a dark cave, and the same uncomfortable feeling that makes us walk faster toward the light that we welcome at the end of the tunnel. If these dark corners and uncomfortable places exist in front of our eyes, then what stops them from existing in the place that counts the most, beyond our sight and in the depth of our thoughts, where the birth of our actions in consummation of our positive and negative thoughts exists? Indeed, the existence of this darkness in the materialistic world is the direct reflection of darkness in our thoughts.

Let me take you on a short journey through the most exciting city ever built. The city with the most beautiful construction, the smoothest roads, the city with all the purity and angelic examples that we have ever known, and the city with the darkest corners and most horrifying places to ever exist. You travel through it many times a day. You are happy and anxious to reach to certain destinations, and sad and afraid of what you may find in the other corners. The good news is that you are its architect and the master planner. All the roads, light, darkness, beauty, and ugliness are built under your direct commandments, and yet you may choose to build a city that you are afraid of traveling through certain portions of it.

Hold the image that you want in your thoughts and it will become reality. The actions that we take are byproducts of our good and bad thoughts. The fears that we experience all have certain common denominators. The doubts, the unknowns, the hopeless feeling of not knowing what to do, the suffocating experience of being in the midst of all emotional events of our lives with no controls, lead us to the dark corners of the city that exists beyond our sight. It appears that we believe that we are constantly victimized by the circumstances that we find trapped in. But it is not circumstances that cause this discomfort and displeasure; indeed, it is how we view ourselves that allows us to react to these circumstances in a certain way.

The key to ridding ourselves of the dark corners and finding the more pleasing parts of our thoughts is to follow the same patterns as if we were to find a new address in our hometown. What are the chances of you successfully finding a destination if the directions are "somewhere in this city and near that vicinity?" Many restless efforts and much energy must be put into finding such a destination, if it's possible at all. Then how is it that we follow the same path of ignorance in finding the lost treasures inside our heads, hoping to find the sources of our fears? The same method of accuracy with a specific address, street, town, state, and all the related helpful information ensures complete success in reaching the desired destination.

There are many consistencies in all aspects of universal laws of creation. From conception to birth to infancy to being a toddler to crawling, walking, and running, the optimum stage of power is a process that is applicable to all aspects of our lives in physical and emotional forms. The huge bully of fear that you run from was conceived, crawled, and walked before becoming the image that frightens you. It is the awareness at early stages that allows us to deal with our fears before they become strong enough to make us powerless. The good news is that facing the bully and investigating all the key elements that created it are chain reactions that allow us to travel down the ladder to its very roots. The key element is to find the links and not be afraid of what we may face at each segment of discovery, knowing that at the end, this formidable infrastructure cannot exist once the parts that have created it are questioned and shattered.

Face the fear and break it down to smaller components so you can see its fallacy. Monitor your thoughts and meditate to slow your brain activity, otherwise it becomes too fast to be detectable. Give yourself specific periods of no-thought activity to break the chain of fearful thoughts. Set small periods every twenty-four hours outside of your sleep pattern where no thought is allowed, regardless of how good or bad it may be. Use guided meditation music if you're not ready to hear the silence yet (such as Holosync or something similar).

Fear is the interpretation of what we know at the time and, in many ways, how we relate to it determines our lifestyle, our path, its magnitude, and how we live our lives. Embrace it in your bosom and hold it tight for all the times to come, since its separation will allow it to grow into the monster that you'll despise.

Enjoy staying in the NOW, where your true unlimited cosmic power and peace is, and remind yourself of the old man's last words before dying: "I have had many troubles in my life, but most of them never happened."

CHAPTER THREE

THE
TRINITY OF SELF

W hat is the very root of our being, our very depth that everything stems from? The part that we do not see yet it makes us the king or the beggar, the master or the slave, the compassionate or the tyrant, the merciful or the savage? The structure that forms us to be or not to be? The scale we must measure up to, and yet our failure and success is based on our deviations from this scale, which was unknowingly made by our thoughts.

From religious points of views to New Age to Buddhism, Taoism, and many other life philosophies—they all have a similar common denominator that consists of the roots of our being in the universal magnitude of creation as defined and enveloped by the trinity of a supreme beginning, the divine consciousness, and the everlasting spirit. Similarities in all forms of our creation dictates that same foundation must exist in the physical dimensions in order to secure our alignments with the universal intentions of our evolution. The same blueprint of the physical forms translates to trinity of self, consisting of our self-image, self-esteem, and self-confidence. These are the ingredients needed to create our heaven or hell as we struggle to maintain the balance between them and bridge the gap between our physical forms and our spiritual existence.

The triangle, the most stable geometric structure, is formed with combination of our self-esteem and self-confidence, building its base and giving stability and support to fulfill self-image at its higher peak.

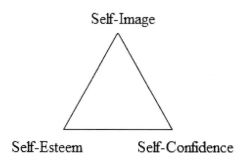

The function of the base components is to fulfill and support completion of the desire that was developed to give us our purpose in the physical form and fulfill our destiny in the larger scheme.

Most of us have a misconception about what each of these categories really mean. Self-confidence is simply the ability and the strength to handle whatever comes our way in daily life and is independent from our physical or financial status. Self-esteem is that deep self-worth that we have for ourselves, supporting the pure fact that we are built from nothing but love and happiness, and that we are worthy of receiving those things at all times.

Simple so far, but not for a long, since the confusing part starts with our self-image. What is it? Where does it come from? How does it start and what makes it change? Is there a right one versus a wrong one? Is there such a thing as a good one versus a bad one? There are seven billion people populating the Earth, with seven billion different faces and not one alike. Amazingly, each has a different self-image unrelated to their physical form and totally different from each other, requiring full support of their bases in order to fulfill their destiny. The self-image must be satisfied in order to provide us the peace that we are searching for. Otherwise, the misalignment of our true self-image versus the false one, forces the ego to step in to replace the void and to provide temporary relief and the mirage of peace. The maintenance of peace among everything else that is happening in our life is our ultimate goal. Our brain is designed to assure us this peace at all costs, even if it is to create the illusion of having it. Confusing, isn't it? But very true!

We are constantly terrorized by different fears in our lives. The optimum level of ingredients that ensure the stability of this base can only be reached when we free ourselves from all fears. Since not that many human beings are able to totally free themselves from that, then it can be assumed that our lives consist of a combination of fears, self-esteem, and self-confidence, and more of one component will result in reduction of the others.

This may be clarified with a real-life example of a yogi. The self-image of a yogi is to be in total peace with no earthly desires and connections. The peak point of his self-triangle is almost in line with the base, creating total harmony. Let's assume that the amount of ego is the area inside this small triangle and is needed for the satisfactory fulfillment of all the components. This ego will be at minimum, since it is only needed to maintain basic functions of the body and the desire for more peace, leading to an optimal level of self-trinity and his perfect balance.

Now, what is ego? It is our earthly companion, which may be explained this way: The night just before you go to sleep, you give up your ego in order to fall asleep; in the morning it is your ego that resumes itself, telling you that you are so-and-so and need to get up and attend whatever you have to accomplish in this life. For a yogi, the minimum ego is healthy and balanced with other ingredients of the trinity of self. However, unfortunately in most cases it is not, and the unbalanced ego is the cause of the limitations and setbacks for our spiritual evolutions.

When the self-image cannot be supported with the available self-esteem and self-confidence, a void is created and the mischievous brain is ready to fulfill its duties by creating those components in the form of a false ego, and rightfully so to protect us from suffering from the desire that was created while knowing that it cannot be met at this time. Let me explain. A second grade teacher, knowing his qualifications supporting his base, has a balanced self-image and ego to teach second graders. However, if the same teacher believes that higher respect and prestige, perhaps as a university professor, are needed in his life in order for him to feel better about himself can create some challenges. Proper goals are healthy in order to develop the bases and reach them, but if our teacher friend starts acting and boasting about himself as a university professor, then the false self-image is maintained by destructive ego disturbing the peace needed to maintain his balance.

The right amount of ego is healthy as long as it can be supported with the other required components, which results in a balanced emotional, spiritual, and psychological life that supports our attainable and reachable self-image. The goal of reaching a different self-image is also healthy and is needed for our progress, but pretending to have one before its time will result in destructive behavior by creating false egos. The best way to describe this is "harmony." We see people who seem totally at peace with who they are, and it appears that they are at a place in their lives where there is harmony. On the other hand, if you look at others whose lives are in chaos, you will easily detect the false self-image, the destructive ego, and the unbalanced components of the self-trinity.

Poetically said, harmony is the pleasure of listening to beautiful music created by the proper tension of a string on an instrument. If it is loose, it will not play; if it is too tight, it will break; but with the right tension, it elevates you to a place where you become detached from time, space, pain, and sorrow, wishing to capture that experience for eternity. The music that you choose to hear and the tension of your life-string are directly proportional to how you balance the components of your self-trinity.

Now, what happens if our second-grade teacher was forced to teach at the preschool? In this case, his self-image is forced lower from what it already was. We feel sympathy for him and say that his ego was hurt. Realistically, it was. It's very simple: He had spent time, enthusiasm, and determination, and had made goals and sacrifices to develop his self-esteem and self-confidence to support his self-image as a second-grade teacher. All of this effort resulted in the proper amount of ego contained inside this triangle, which is balanced for the time being. When the self-image is lowered from what it was before, then the excess ego that was created inside this triangle has no place to go other than outside of his self-trinity that he is currently operating at. This will result in depression, shame, doubt, detachment, and feelings of failure. All of these are in preparation of reducing his self-esteem and self-confidence to support the lower self-image and find balance in supporting the peace needed in his life.

Does this mean that a university professor has a higher self-esteem and self-confidence and is a better person than a second-grade teacher? Of course not, they both have the same values and rights as human beings in society, and both can be happy with their positions in life as long as they have a balanced triangle. The value of the self-image is not determined by society or the prestige that one may hold, but it is a personal choice to accomplish in order to give someone the satisfaction they need to feel deserving of happiness. A second-grade teacher may feel much more confident and may have much higher self-esteem than a professor who feels inadequate at his position in life, regardless of what the society may think.

All of this sounds very interesting, but what purpose does knowing all of this have in our individual growth? Well, if you desire to find out why you are not reaching where you want to go and your search for answers has led you to reading this book and this chapter, then it is time for you to know all the above and to compare that with your past and present events in an effort to manage your future.

Think about all the times that you made choices with unhappy results. Would have you made the same choices if you had more information and if you could estimate the outcome of your actions based on certain existing patterns that you were able to detect? There is a reason for everything that happens in our lives. Each experience has profound messages that become apparent in the long term. Patience is the antidote to stop us from reacting to situations whose reasons for existence will be revealed at later dates.

How do you define yourself? How many times do certain lessons have to be repeated before you learn? Before you see the patterns and connect the dots that show you the same situations has existed before? Do you need one lesson to learn, or do lessons have to be repeated over and over again before you realize that the cure is not in suppressing and ignoring, but in stopping it from happening by changing direction and recognizing the universal lessons that exist to guide us to the right path?

Maintaining the balance of self-trinity is not a destination; it is a journey that is felt, touched, desired, meditated on, and lived at all times along the way. Happiness and bliss are not destinations that we aim to reach; they are the quality of the journey that we travel at every moment. You isolate yourself from the goals since they are the things that you desire far away from yourself, and you hope that you will get to them at a certain time of your life. If peace, happiness, and bliss are your goals, then what will you have along the way when you have not reached them yet?

Many of us go from one fix to the other, searching for that optimal level of accomplishment that will give us the maximum pleasure that we are looking for. The craving and the vacuum that pulls us to emptiness become larger and larger each time, contradictory to expectation. The patterns are the same regardless of what substance is being used. Shame, hate, jealousy, judgment, and many of our other behaviors are in many ways the same as drugs, alcohol, sex, gambling, and other vices used by addicts. The triangular structure of the tyrant or the compassionate is the same body disguised with different masks fulfilling the desires of self-images.

Now the reasons for the complexity of this element of the self-trinity and its importance become more and more apparent. The roots for each behavior can be investigated by putting it at the peak of the triangle and finding the relations between self-esteem, self-confidence, and ego as they apply to that condition. Our self-image at any present moment dictates how we respond to certain situations, and in many ways the combination of several of these images will set the foundation for our future goals and personalities as we age. What makes us want to become whatever it is that we are aiming for is built-up of layers and layers of these images forming and reforming to what is intended to give us the peace and happiness that we desperately seek.

How could finding yourself and wanting to know the reasons for your actions be so difficult? Indeed, it may be very simple: "When the student is ready, the lesson will be, and the teacher will appear." Or better said, the lesson has always been there and is only "seen" when the reason for wanting the lesson are completed and the prize is won. Simply said, it is similar to walking in the street and observing people as they pass by. You may see acquaintances and people you have met before, and you greet them as they pass; you see friends of friends and recognize who they are and wave as you continue your walk; and then your arms open up, your heart pounds with excitement and pleasure, and you run to embrace a close friend, the one you feel a connection with and recognize due to many close encounters of your pasts, which developed the attachment for this reaction. We recognize teachers in the same manner once our thoughts have created bonds with what we are looking for in life.

Hold the image that you want in your thoughts, and it will be materialized in every form that you desire. Somehow the base will develop itself to support the self-image. The climax for this balance of trinity is only accomplished when the proper ego is developed to support all the components. Take any of your emotions and put them at the peak to evaluate your components, and you will find the keys to your reactions and behaviors, likes and dislikes in every situation.

Let's put this concept to work. Pick an emotion or behavior that confuses you when you react to it in a way that is pleasing or displeasing. How about shame? Let's analyze the other ingredients of the self-trinity when self-image is acting shamefully. Shame is an attitude that we have about ourselves. It is a form of wishing that you were invisible. It is a form of emotional suicide to destroy yourself, since the fear of detachment and non-acceptance from whatever you were hoping to be is threatened. Well, the fingerprints of the bases are very clear. The self-esteem is greatly reduced because the cause of this feeling of shame has triggered feelings and emotions that you do not deserve love anymore. The self-confidence is very weak because the cause of this shame has led you to believe that whatever is happening cannot be handled and is beyond your capabilities. The ego is confused and is desperately trying to increase itself to maintain the area that was inside this triangle based on the self-image that you had previously developed for yourself, but it's constantly being pulled down because the bases have been reduced. The end result is that your self-trinity has no option but to reduce itself to a smaller triangle. The differences of the two areas inside the two triangles of what you were and what you are represent the shame that's being felt due to the reduction of the egos.

It is greatly important to know the structure of our psyche in order to recognize dots and find patterns. The cure is not found by looking for the remedies, but by studying the disease first. In order to defend against a destructive weapon, you must first master it; once mastered, the weapon's weaknesses and the counteractions will magically appear. At the same time, the focus must remain on the solution without becoming preoccupied with the problem.

Our society has conditioned us to look for shortcuts and to accomplish tasks in faster and faster time periods. The increase of production has made us boast about our success, but recognizing and investigating the byproducts of our actions makes us wonder whether the net results have justified the benefits. We have given up our capacity for patience and have accustomed ourselves to immediate results. Our behavior and emotions have developed expectations for immediate responses. The quantum leap from the relief of the good intentions of using drugs for temporary relief to allow for recovery and healing has transformed into permanent solutions that allow the causes to go undetected. Our magazines and publications showing the demand and likes and dislikes of the masses have moved from "Life" and "Us" and "We" to the recent publications of "Me" and "Self" in the last century. Going from "life" to "me" is not a trick for profit caused by journalism, but it is a clear indication of how society's thought patterns and interests have shifted from life to self.

It appears that we have succeeded in unknowingly reversing the process of our evolvement. It has been said that human evolvement has four stages. First, we direct our attention to our physical shell and preoccupy ourselves with how beautiful and strong we can be. Second, our efforts are focused on how many materialistic things we can gather. The third step is to move away from our selfish motives and look into how we can be of service to others. The last step is to realize that we are not physical beings having spiritual experiences, that in actuality it is the other way around.

The importance of self-trinity is amplified even more by recognizing the steps toward spiritual evolution. The path from "life" to "me" will lead to destruction if the focus of this interest is anything other than investigation of our personal behaviors for better understanding of ourselves and utilization of this knowledge to promote greater understanding of love and enlightenment. The roots of all behaviors emanate from love and are caused by having it or not. The laws of nature have shown us that we cannot give away things we do not have.

Simply said, the bundle of joy is the self-trinity, which becomes larger and larger with its proper balance and shall turn into love for ourselves, which will overflow all around us.

It is important to recognize the fine line between "self" and the "selfish," where in the name of the crusade to find the self, we may behave selfishly.

Somehow, there is a desire in each of us to find ourselves in this physical experience called life. Some are born with knowledge of that cosmic self that beats their hearts, and they have no further desire to search. For some, it takes a few years to find the true self. For others, it takes many years, and for a select few, it will never happen in one lifetime.

Finding the self requires exploration of all aspects of the self. Along this path of inquiry, many of us doubt that we are a drop in the ocean. When a drop of the ocean misunderstands itself to be the ocean, it separates itself and evaporates. Eventually all forms of water find themselves back in the ocean since there is no other path.

The key to finding the self and the time that elapses to accomplish that lies in the understanding of the selfish.

It is impossible to reach a destination with a broken compass. It is impossible to search for truth with a lie and expect to find the absolute truth. It is impossible to look for the self through anything other than its absolute essence of love and find it. When we look for the self through fear, we find selfishness, and when we look for the self through its true essence of love, we truly find that too.

There may be a fine line between the self and the selfish, since holding on to all that we believe to be the self with fear creates the selfish in this path of exploration to find the self.

Since we are the observer of this experience, and in a way the center of attention, then it makes sense to want to experience all that self can experience. For whatever reason, our attraction directs us to include or dismiss these desired experiences at different levels. Some are eliminated before they become a thought. Some are eliminated through our thoughts, and some are eliminated only through satisfaction of the relative physical experiences.

Swami Rama's *Living with Himalayan Masters* tells the story of a young yogi who was sent to a master to learn from him. On the way to the master's cave, the young yogi sees some gold coins at the well. He picks them up as he gets his water. Afterward he thinks to himself, *I am a yogi. What use would I have for gold coins?* He puts them back and continues to the master's cave. The master welcomes him but tells him that he is not ready to learn from the master yet. He asks the young yogi, "Why did you pick up the gold coins at the well?" The yogi responds, "But I put them back." The master says, "It has no importance that you put them back. What is important is that you had the desire that attracted you to them in the first place."

> "He should lift up the self by the Self and not sink into the selfish; for the self is the only friend of the Self, and its only foe. . . . When a man has mastered himself, he is perfectly at ease in cold, in heat, in pleasure or pain, in honor or in disgrace. . . He looks impartially on all. Those who love him or hate him, his kinsmen, his enemies, his friends, the good, and also the wicked." — BHAGAVAD GITA

We should also recognize how our identity sculpts itself by peer pressure in an attempt to prove that the imposter who has been born is the absolute.

Most of us are familiar with identity theft and have experienced it directly or know of someone who has been exposed to it. Basically, the thief steals your identity by pretending to be you so they can gain from this fictitious misrepresentation, which is considered stealing.

However, there is another version of this identity theft that has been going on for centuries without anyone ever holding the thieves responsible for their actions or punishing them or asking for restitution, or at least a simple acknowledgement that this has been going on and a promise to stop it.

The victim of this identity theft is each of us living in a society that requires performance against a certain standard. The thief is the ego that has deceived us into believing that we are something different than what we truly are. The loss is all the moments when we believe that we are far from true essence of joy and happiness as we experience sorrow. Also, the loss is the false belief that we are less than whole.

We are born with our true identity, knowing who we truly are, how powerful we are, and how limitless we can be. We are born to enjoy flying, feeling the wind under our wings as we soar to the sky, but then we're told that we were born to limp like the others before us. Indeed, the pleasure of not having pain is great, but why impose self-directed pain in the first place? Why put self-driven obstacles in our path and then try to avoid them, slowing ourselves down to less than our potentials?

How do we identify this thief and stop this process, so we can resume being our true self?

One of the most common techniques to stop identify theft is that at the start of the transaction; there are agreements made and questions put in place that only the two parties would know. Such as, what was the name of your first pet? What is your mother's middle name? What was the name of the first car you owned?

The same techniques are available to detect the ego when it attempts to hijack your identity by giving you the idea that you are something different. There was an agreement made when we came as spiritual beings having physical experiences. Any two-year-old would know that and is fully aware of the agreement. However, as the thief stole our identity, we soon transitioned into physical beings persuaded by the ego, hoping to have little special glimpses of those spiritual experiences.

To identify the thief, ask these questions the next time you are guided to do something by that quiet voice inside:

- Will this be a loving act toward someone or something? Is it without conditions?
- Will this make me more kind than right?
- Will this allow me to help versus to rule?
- Will this allow me to change, to learn, and to be refined if different than others' expectations without lessening my self-evaluation?
- Will this make me more compassionate?

If the answers to these questions are "yes," then the guidance is genuine. If the answers are "no," then the thief's master plan is silently in action.

In order to evaluate all aspects of the trinity of self, one must consider that things may not appear as they seem. Are things truly what they appear to be or does our perception of what we think them to be, or think they should be, give them the reality of what we assume we want them to be? Based on that assumption, many other thoughts will follow as we build walls to protect what we believe is reality. The belief is nothing other than a thought after thought, affirmed by self-interpreted feedbacks becoming a self-fulfilled prophecy.

We give these thoughts personalities to include or to exclude them as we categorize them based on these assumptions, as we put them in one of our preconceived boxes to be stereotyped for that category. Very soon our brain becomes so efficient that it controls our behavior and reactions toward others by immediately putting them in one of those boxes based on preconceived notions and prearranged and predetermined ideas.

Our brain draws a conclusion that with the slightest signal, someone or something qualifies to be put in one box where that may be considered good, wonderful, great, friendly, and innocent, but the other box means terrible, horrifying, enemy, monstrous, unfriendly, and guilty.

A child's first experience with a spider through observing the reactions of their caretakers, siblings, or others can put the spider in the box to be feared for all the years to come, or the box that encourages the child to become a zoologist in hope of saving all the spiders in the world. Once the box is made, every subsequence experience with spiders will create the anticipated preconceived outcome automatically, without further exploration of why and how it was determined to be that way.

"We do not see things as they are, we only see things as we are!"

Living with Himalayan Masters describes how masses can be fooled by looking for solutions outside of themselves, even when searching for a guru that may appear to fall into that category of our predetermined box.

There was a lonely laundryman who had a donkey. He would go around and gather all his customers' laundry on top of his donkey to wash. His donkey was the main source of his livelihood, his companion, and basically all he believed that he had.

One day his donkey fell to the ground and died. The man was shocked by this unbearable loss of his donkey and sat down on a street corner in despair. He was immobile, appearing to sit in an erect position without moving at all. As people walked by, they noticed this man sitting there in a meditative state without moving for a long time.

Only advanced yogis and masters can sit in a meditative state without moving for several hours. Untrained yogis cannot maintain that position without taking breaks. *Samadhi* is a meditative state in which a yogi sits in the same position for several hours focused on a single thought, where they gain universal knowledge or enlightenment, which is taught to their disciples.

People started paying more attention to this man who had sat there in a still position with his eyes closed for a long time. Very soon word spread that there was a master yogi sitting in the same position, meditating. People gathered around him and put fruit and gifts by his feet to celebrate this saint. They awaited his profound comeback and the messages of universal knowledge that would bring. Even other yogis came and sat by his feet once they heard of this master yogi sitting in the state of *Samadhi* for many hours. They were all anxious to learn what he would teach them upon his return.

After many hours of anticipation, the laundryman opened his eyes to the crowd of people awaiting his words of wisdom and said, "Where is my donkey?"

Nothing appears as it seems to be, regardless of what box the observer has chosen to put that condition in. "Change the way you look at things and the things you look at change".-Wayne Dyer.

Evaluate and question all the boxes that you have created along your life's path. Recognize that love has no boxes and compassion connects all the boxes into one.

CHAPTER FOUR

THE LIGHTS WITHIN, STRUGGLE WITH SELF

The lights within shine through all the windows. As I walk in a crowded street and observe people, sometimes I wonder what it is inside each of us beyond all the façade that still reaches out through all the layers and layers of disguise. I wonder at the energy and the beauty that resonates from some people and the hatred and fear that cries for help from the others. Not even the most beautiful clothing and jewelry can stop that glance into someone's eyes which shows you the path to their most inner secrets. The insecurities, the fears, the love, the pain, the shame, the joy, the happiness, and the sadness somehow reflect out. But which is it? The beauty inside that, once seen through your inner eyes, allows recognition of the same in others? Or the attitude of others toward you that forms how you behave and what you are accepting to be—you?

The Picture of Dorian Gray is a classic movie that can change your life forever once watched and understood. The most handsome, rich, and good-hearted man has his portrait painted by an artist with a mystic power. Somehow the painting captures his physical appearance and his soul, which were the same at the time. The young Dorian decides to experience the dark side of life and starts drinking, lying, and visiting prostitutes, even deceiving a woman and causing her to kill herself. He notices that the picture is changing. He becomes more and more obsessed with how his soul is changing and, finally frightened of looking at the painting, hides it. Amazingly, he was not aging and his physical appearance had stayed young and handsome as ever, while the portrait displayed a horrifying physical image of his real self.

If only we could see the changes in our true being, that inner person who watches everything we do and who bears the scars. Only then could we have an opportunity to change ourselves and align our life before it is too late. And then again, maybe not. Maybe that inner desire to do whatever it is that drives us is stronger than paying attention to all the signals along the way. Dorian found that out just before he died, but it was too late.

Learning requires time, time requires patience, and patience allows us to proceed wisely toward whatever it is that our thoughts are set for. If time and effort are put into changing ourselves for better or worse, then to undo the destructive behavior once we recognize it as being hazardous to our journey in life will require much more time and patience than what was put into creating it in the first place. Somehow the pruning that is required to keep our lives pleasing to our inner sights requires much more work than creating the weeds that have grown wildly out of control.

It will be an amazing moment of realization when we recognize that our struggles are not based on "you against them," but totally enveloped around "you against you." The radiance from you to the outside world stems from the conclusion of certain attitudes against yourself.

Look around you. What do you see beyond your visions? People, objects, sceneries, actions, and reactions to all the events present themselves as a silent movie with a subtitle. The images exist, but the interpretations of the many events create the subtitle of the movie of life stemming from your points of view. Amazingly, the same movie through another person's eyes will have entirely different interpretations and subtitles.

The reality of the movie cannot be denied and, in many cases, may not be subject to interpretation due to clarity of the circumstances. However, there are many instances where different viewers will create their own realities.

How could a person who is cruel to himself be compassionate to others, and how could a person who is gentle with himself violate others? The religious belief that what comes out of the mouth is what is important, and not the other way around, has been with us for over two thousand years, but it has not been completely understood and practiced when it was used to emphasize the reasons behind fasting. The physical fasting intended to be practiced in different religions on the so-called Sabbath or other occasions was not meant to deny ourselves food and stop ourselves from nourishing the physical body. It was intended to create the strength needed for our spiritual evolvement. What comes out of the mouth is the combination of all you are—the beliefs, the fears, the love, hate, anger, and compassion bundled within yourself.

What an ingenious idea to tame what comes out of our mouths, indicating what is in our hearts by controlling what is going in through our mouths.

Historically, the proper method of fasting has never been to only stop the eating on physical levels, but to refrain from all thoughts and actions hazardous to our enlightenment reinforced by the discomfort of hunger. Sounds familiar, doesn't it? It has been proven over and over again that many of our abusive behaviors toward ourselves and others result in physical pains. This is only a simple duplication of what our creation and nature has already prepared for us. The majority of physical illnesses are caused by certain self-inflicted destructive behaviors and thoughts.

It was once assumed that many of our illnesses were created by viruses and germs attacking our bodies. For centuries, we blamed many external sources for our health issues and deaths. The latest research has proven that this is not the case. The culprits to blame for many of our discomforts and problems were inside us long before their active states, in a dormant stage. It has been proven that the reduction of immune systems allows these viruses and germs to become active and hazardous to our health.

Similar patterns exist in our behavioral and psychological construction. The viruses and germs are the events and experiences that we face on a daily basis and have been exposed to over the years. They simply exist since they have occurred and been observed by us. Their existence alone does not cause a problem, since the interpretation and processing of this information and the method that will be chosen to deal with it becomes the key to our happiness and evolvement or misery and struggle.

Simply said, self-confidence is our psyche's immune system. Processing the same information can have different impacts and results at different levels of our self-confidence. Regardless of how we choose to utilize this information, the obvious fact remains that higher self-confidence facilitates a more pleasant mental state, peace, tranquility, and accelerated evolvement. However, self-doubt is a shaky foundation for stable behavior and will create anxiety, fear, judgment, hate, and sorrow, which delays our spiritual growth and accelerates deterioration of our physical body.

To love or not to love, that is indeed the question. To forgive or to hate, to care or not to care, and many of our other decisions all stem from our level of self-confidence. The confidence is developed and energized by our self-acceptance. Higher struggle with our self-acceptance has a direct relation to our lower self-confidence. Then the struggle that seems never-ending will continue. You against you, again and again, will soon become a familiar voice of rejection. The bond that is developed between these two polarities will create the comfort of accepting this struggle as a way of life. Self-doubt becomes an acceptable familiar face in all our decisions.

Soon, we become our worst enemies by setting the stage for our failures. It is as simple as believing that if you are surrounded by water in the middle of a lake, you shall drown. You struggle and swim, looking for the shore that is far beyond your physical strength to reach, and never entertain that the water may only be up to your waist and that you could be saved by simply standing.

The self-recovery that is planted into our existence ensures that our heads remain above the same water that is about to suffocate us; it will demand our survival, will demand our struggle with that which has disturbed our peace. Our freedom comes from the moments in life when we have the opportunity to taste the pleasure of being ourselves, not driven by self-doubt but living in total self-confidence. Being simply at peace and indeed not with others, but with ourselves. The peace within has no other reflection other than peace with everything and everyone that one comes in contact with.

Indeed, the sun will surely rise when we recognize that the source of this self-confidence is rooted deep within us, and all we need to access its unlimited potential is a willing heart. The desire to understand the "whys" and "hows" of the things that continue repeating themselves in the same patterns and are considered disruptive to our peace of mind. The courage to look in and not be afraid of what we may find since the love we have for ourselves will provide strength and courage. To recognize that the love for ourselves is far beyond the mask of arrogance that portrays itself in cold detached ways to protect one who lacks the warmth of the unconditional love. Dorian Gray will surely attest after his experience that the beauty inside is independent from the shell outside.

To give a man a fish will feed him for a day; to teach him how to fish will satisfy him for a lifetime. To blame others for our challenges will satisfy us through the mirage of distraction for a short while. However, to take responsibility for our actions—and understanding that at some point in our lives we become responsible for our actions—will satisfy us for a lifetime. The satisfaction comes from the understanding that the one who holds others responsible for his actions will feel more and more powerless as his audience grows larger and larger.

Building our self-confidence is no different than building our physical body. Unfortunately, the method of detection is not as easy as looking in the mirror.

Two people with identical physical sizes and capabilities interested in developing their biceps may use different strategies to do so. One may rely on everyone else to make this happen for him, such as using other people to perform different exercises on his arms because he is not willing to endure the discomfort that may be required to accomplish such a task. Exhaustive hours of physiotherapy, massage, acupuncture, etc., will have poor results at the end of the term, but this person does not understand the poor results because he holds all the others responsible for his failure.

However, the other person who holds himself responsible for maximizing the strength of his biceps will take the following actions:

1. Learn as much as possible about the structure that he is intending to develop

2. Study the best methods to accomplish such a task

3. Search and utilize the best diet in order to assist and nourish this body part

4. Use trainers and teachers to learn the best ways

5. Be disciplined to maintain the regular regiment of the programs needed

6. Be patient to appreciate his developments one step at the time

This person is empowered by the strength that this independence will give him to accomplish what is at hand and recognizes that the outcome is totally directed by his decisions and actions. He recognizes the power within.

Once you recognize that we hold the key to our happiness or misery, then you may be comforted to know that this is the best first step toward recognizing that you are fine just the way you exist at this point of time regardless of what you believe.

There is nothing broken within you that requires fixing. Everything has its intended place and time frame within creation.

It has been said that the three challenges each of us faces every day are to send love in response to hate, to admit when we are wrong, and to defend the absentee.

Maybe understanding the anatomy of each of these will help us understand ourselves better in dealing with them, hoping that our path will be led by the knowledge that is gained when exploring these three encounters and leading to uphold them in lieu of defying them.

1. *To send love in response to hate*

We are born to love unconditionally but somehow along the path of growing up, we learn to measure everything. Very soon we create an unspoken invisible bar for how to measure the love toward ourselves and its reflections to others, known as conditional love. I love you only if you behave in a certain way that is pleasing to me. I hate you if you behave a different way. I wait to see how you treat me before I make up my mind about how I feel about you. There are unlimited variables that can influence the outcome of this measuring strategy.

Since the heart loves and the left brain provides all the reasons to doubt it, we never find the absolute point of measurement to have the right answer under all conditions. The brain is equipped to provide unlimited combination of reasons. Loving with directions from the mischievous brain will never lead to unconditional love because there will always be a reason to protect the ego with conditions.

When we recognize that love is generated from self to self and is provided by that unlimited source that provides that energy without prejudice, we no longer have a measuring bar that moves based on conditions. We no longer look for love in all places subject to variations. We find the absolute as being unconditional love. In that state, the only measuring bar is from self to self as aligned with the energy that beats all our hearts, affirming that love must overcome regardless of opinion of others.

What is it about children that attracts and magnetizes us? Even if it is for a short moment of freedom from all the burdens that have enveloped us. Even for a short grasp of looking into their eyes and finding no struggle other than the pulling force of their unlimited love. The clarity in their eyes stemming from no resistance, no prejudged notions, no influence by others, breaks the barriers put up by even the most hard-hearted human beings, making them like children again. Indeed, it was said many centuries ago that you shall not enter heaven unless you become like a child again. Whatever the intentions have been for our beginning and end, our life and death, our happiness and sadness, and our love and hate lie within maintaining that childish wisdom and attitude without allowing it to be polluted by society.

2. To admit when we are wrong

Water, ice, and vapor are all considered to be the same substance, however they behave differently in different environments and temperatures. To be wrong is subject to evaluation and interpretation of all respective conditions. To hurt someone is wrong, but a justified war to protect may be considered to be the right thing to do. In order to define wrongness, we must establish what is considered to be right at that moment.

However, there is a measuring bar that has no environment, that has no barrier and produces the same response under all conditions. It may be considered the absolute and is called kindness. Under this condition, the focus shifts from being right to being kind, and will act independent of any concerns about being wrong.

3. *To defend the absentee*

To defend the absentee requires seizing the need to gain approval of others and acting independent of their opinions.

In the name of searching for another person's approval or acceptance, we may elect to choose the path of silence in response to something that we may find to be untrue.

When we choose silence in lieu of defending the absentee, we have chosen to numb ourselves from the hurt that they may have been subjected to if they were present. The only gate that allows us to understand another person's pain is compassion. Defending the absentee will require acting with compassion.

It appears that the three most common daily challenges leading to dis-ease will transform to being at ease when we act with unconditional love, kindness, and compassion.

How many times per day do we ask ourselves and wonder, "How could I possibly behave that way?"

There is an old saying that goes, "We all have ten minutes in twenty-four hours that we act like lunatics, but the lucky ones are the ones whose ten minutes happen when they are asleep."

Sometimes we react to events in ways that we consider totally out of character. Later, we usually ponder with guilt and comments like, "Who was that? Where did that come from? I hate that part of me! How could I possibly think or act that way?"

The simple answer is this. You can never get apple juice from an orange, so as much as you may dislike your response, somehow it was imported and allowed to be stored inside you with roots that may not be easily detectable.

The best way to get these feelings out is to first recognize that you have them and then accept what was done so you can forgive yourself. Continue by filling yourself with all that you desire to have, using repetitive quotations, mantras, books, music, supporting programs, and attitudes conducive with the desired behavior until they overflow and flush out the undesired behavior and beliefs.

There is always a gap between the event and our reaction to it. Our power to choose will always lie in that gap. When our choices come from security and love, we are energetically pleased with our response, and when they come from insecurity and fear, they seem to be foreign to our universal default and we interpret them as unpleasant and a part of that ten minutes when we wished we had been asleep.

What about when we doubt our existence, our goodness, and our values by constantly searching for the answer to the constantly pinging problem of being good enough?

The majority of people fall in one of the two groups of "I am not good enough" or "I am so afraid of not being good enough that I need a big ego to cover it up by pretending that I am more than good enough."

So, when will the viscous cycle of this question end, and where did it ever begin?

In order to be less than something, there must be a measuring bar. The measuring bar requires judgment and will require left brain activities that establish some kind of analysis relating to peer pressure of the surroundings that reinforced certain guidelines to fit into a certain category. Parents, teachers, coaches, other adults, friends, and our social lives define this measuring bar as we react to them in search of love and acceptance from those we look up to.

Children are born to be loved and cared for. However, as parents and caregivers fail to provide that environment due to their own issues, children are forced to take action and fix this imbalance using their limited resources. They start developing the attitude that *if I do better in school, if I'm nicer, politer, better at sports, if I win more, etc., these issues will change and I will have the loving and caring environment that I desire.* Since this was not the real reason for others' misbehavior to begin with, the results are usually not favorable. Children view this as failure, so they try harder.

Eventually they believe that regardless of how much they have won and how much they have accomplished, they had failed in fixing this issue. They believe that they have failed reaching that measuring bar, and if they had been able to reach that, it would have fixed whatever was obstructing that unconditional love, care, support, and protection. As adults, they will always feel that they were never good enough, and the vicious cycle continues. (For example: *If I am good enough, my mom will spend more time with me, my dad will not be as mad, my parents will not fight, they will not use alcohol, they will not be abusive, they will be better, they will pay more attention to me, etc.*)

Our misconception of this distorted measuring bar will impact our entire life until we realize that it is a mirage. The absolute universal measuring bar has no bar since its essence is compassion, which glues our left and right brain and cannot have anything else other than understanding. Since there was no bar to begin with, then the entire question of "good enough" becomes a fallacy of our interpretation at its core. Those parents and other individuals had issues independent from our state of goodness and unrelated to what we had tried to do.

Mother Teresa beautifully states what the measuring bar would be, if any, in her poem, "The Final Analysis":

People are often unreasonable, illogical, and self-centered. Forgive them anyway.

If you are kind, people may accuse you of selfish ulterior motives. Be kind anyway.

If you are successful, you will win some false friends and some true enemies. Succeed anyway.

If you are honest and frank, people may cheat you. Be honest and frank anyway.

What you spend years building, someone could destroy overnight Build anyway.

If you find serenity and happiness, they may be jealous. Be happy anyway.

The good you do today, people will often forget tomorrow. Do good anyway.

Give the world the best you have, and it may never be enough. Give the best you've got anyway.

You see, in the final analysis it is all between you and God; it was never between you and them anyway.

After all is said and done, do we really know what we want? So, what do you really want?

In your personal life or in your interactions with others, have you ever realized that sometimes you do not know what you really want, but it seems that all you want is the opposite of the other person's wanting?

This can be a personal relationship, business interactions, casual interactions with others, political views, or any other occasion where an individual may have an opportunity to express their views. This escalates to be habitual, and very soon it becomes a habit of constantly being argumentative and looking for opportunities to hold opposing views.

When you notice this behavior, it will be comical to ask the other person, "What do you really want?" You will soon find out that the answer is, "I do not know, but I want whatever is the opposite of what you or others want."

Our daily attitude and energetic behavior toward life is mainly divided into four categories:

1. *You are happy and want to be happy.* This is our universal default, and it is great to be at this state. Dis-ease cannot exist at this level because you cannot find dis-ease in ease, which comes from happiness and joy of being at this high energetic vibration. It seems as though you have no body and you enjoy every moment of life to the fullest. You are inspired at all times. Thoreau said, "Our greatest moments are when we live our dreams awake." When you are at this state, stay in it, milk it to the maximum, and promote it so you can be a lighthouse for others. Do not listen to anyone and do not change anything!

2. *You are happy and want to be unhappy.* This is easy and appears to be the path of least resistance for many due to their wrong conditioning and adoption of the environment. Listen to negative news, gossip, be hateful and jealous, cheat and lie, want less for others than for yourself, watch soap operas, talk negatively about things, and more. Very quickly you will find yourself with fewer reasons to be happy, and you will find more and more things to be unhappy about.

3. *You are unhappy and want to be unhappy.* The universe and flow of nature is based on ease of flow and energy. Any kind of dis-ease is considered to flow upstream and is not congruent with the flow of universe. Since happiness comes with fluency of energy, unhappiness stems from the dis-ease and discomfort of experiencing life. One may say that being unhappy is not the norm, so our interpretation of that unhappy experience will eventually correct itself to continue with the natural flow of happiness. The

first step to correct this misalignment is to simply and humbly remain unhappy if you believe that it is what you want. The ease of getting what you want will encourage you to be happy about it and will eventually return you to your natural, default state of happiness. Sometimes the best way to allow irritation to pass is to remain in that state of irritation without resistance to allow it to correct itself.

4. *You are unhappy and want to be happy.* This is when you are ready to do what is needed. To learn and to move forward, to get out of the box. To stop acting per what is expected by the environment, to act beyond it, to grow. Steel is folded many times through the heat and cold to be as strong and sharp as needed to cut through anything. This is when you recognize how blessed you are to have gained this profound experience of unhappiness, which has prepared you for your ultimate goal of happiness. At this stage the student is ready, and at each corner of their path, a teacher will appear with pleasant and profound lessons that were never apparent before. This is the state of bliss where you recognize that your only goal is to remain happy, and you will no longer seek any reasons to be otherwise. Ask yourself again with this new understanding, "What do I really want?"

What would you do with the portrait of your soul if you were able to look at it every day? Would you display it for all to see and enjoy at every moment of your life, or would you hide it away like the young Dorian Gray, because you are afraid of what you may see?

Whichever you choose will no longer be protected by the bliss of ignorance, since you now have the wisdom that yes, you are blessed or cursed with having such a portrait. Listen to the profound sound of silence and the white canvas will appear. Stop resisting; let go of the fear of what you may find, be willing to observe, and vague images will take form. Be willing to recognize the path from self-hate to compassion and acceptance, and the final strokes are completed, allowing you to observe and enjoy the reasons for your being in the most beautiful portrait that has always been awaiting your recognition of its perfection.

CHAPTER FIVE

LOVE AND HATE ARE SELF-GENERATED

Would it matter, If the whole world hated you and you loved yourself? Or, would it matter if the whole world loved you and you hated yourself?

Indeed, love and hate are self-generated once we recognize the roots of the technology of creation, but do we really know what love is and what the differences are when conditions are imposed? Do we know how its lack in response to fear has a byproduct leading to hate at its opposite extreme?

Most of us use the phrase "I love you" many times every day and rarely get an opportunity to investigate our intention to see what we really mean by that—either "I love you unconditionally" or "I love you when you act in a way that is pleasing to me."

We consider both of them love and refer to them many times to show our affection toward others; however, which one do we really believe in and practice? Since our extreme opposite polarities are defined as love and fear, then it may be safe to assume that any mixture of fear with love will create conditional love.

As children we are born with energetic unconditional love, but something changes as we grow up. We start deviating from that energetic love to a love that is established through our feelings. Since feelings are usually responses that we get from something or someone, all feeling-driven responses will make that love conditional. This will soon shift our interpretation that when we feel good, we offer unconditional love, and when we don't feel good, we offer conditional love. This is mainly caused by shifting away from the truth that all love is from self to self, since you cannot give away something that you do not have.

Since we define all our experiences in comparison to the only measuring bar we know—ourselves—first, then unconditional love must be recognized and offered internally from self to self before it can be extended to anyone else.

Hafiz said, "Even after all this time, the sun never says to the Earth, 'You owe me.' Look what happens with a love like that. It lights the whole sky."

The path to loving more is to care less through acceptance and removal of all judgment, allowing others to be themselves with assurance that you love them regardless of conditions, regardless of what they decide is unconditional love. Accepting ourselves and others just the way we are facilitates removing all self-imposed conditions that cause diversions.

We may say that the door from conditional love to unconditional love is forgiveness and self-acceptance, since the fear that has imposed the conditions must be left behind as we enter into the new recognition that there is only one form of love and it has no conditions.

"Unconditional Love starts from within. It is not dependent upon anyone or anything. Unconditional Love is eternal, transcending both time and space. It does not have any expectations or restrictions attached to it whatsoever. It's completely without all limitation. There is an endless supply of unconditional love inside each of us, of which we can use to create the world and lives of our dreams. We all have the power to dream a new world full of unconditional Love, Peace, and Unity for all into being here and now. To awake into this new tomorrow, follow your heart, believe in yourself and trust in love." — PAUL ADKINS

It appears that love leading to peace can only flow when acceptance is present, otherwise it may never truly be experienced. When acceptance occurs naturally, there is no recognition of it, there is no resistance, and it seems that we have accepted it by default as we move peacefully forward. However, when something undesired is experienced, we try to convince ourselves to accept that, and acceptance by default is no longer experienced, as it leads to many struggles and disappointments, causing sadness and sorrow. We find acceptance under those conditions to be interpreted and construed as giving up, forfeiting the desire, allowing whatever wrong is happening to continue negatively, admitting defeat, feeling apathy, and more.

Acceptance is simply the energetic response of the universe clarifying that the time to materialize our desire has not arrived yet. Consider a merry-go-round: you must run at the same speed of the merry-go-round before you can get on, otherwise it will bump you off. You may try once or twice and slow down or stop and then try again until you can get on and enjoy the ride. Acceptance is that slowing down or stopping delay that synchronizes the vibrations to ensure success, and it is contradictory to its misconception of being defeated.

It simply states that I am joyful as I am now and accept that I will need to continue working on my desire and be happy at this moment, under these conditions, until I reach my goals. Acceptance is the key to recovery.

We shift from living for tomorrow or pondering about the past when we accept ourselves exactly as we are, in exactly this moment and we begin to appreciate today.

In his book *Man's Search for Meaning*, Viktor Frankl shares his experience as a prisoner in a Nazi Germany concentration camp during World War II. It was his acceptance of the merciless conditions that allowed him to retain his energy to keep his desire alive. He knew that he had to survive to share his story, so he could be part of the force to stop such horror from happening again.

Acceptance allows willingness to flourish. Prerequisite to any form of acceptance is willingness. In vibrational hierarchy to joy and peace, reason allows acceptance to take place. One may say that the three musketeers leading us to love are willingness, acceptance, and reason.

Eckhart Tolle said, "Accept—then act. Whatever the present moment contains, accept it as if you had chosen it. Always work with it, not against it. . . . This will miraculously transform your whole life."

The power of acceptance is the energy that allows transformation to occur. Change comes when we act beyond our norm, our comfort level, and our environement. Acceptance allows the energy wasted on regret, hate, and sorrow to be retained and redirected for transformation.

> *"Acceptance does not mean resignation. It means understanding that something is what it is and there's got to be a way through it."* — MICHAEL J. FOX

So, if acceptance allows love to flow, then what stops love from flowing? Our true essence of being is the perfection of our maintenance of peace. Any fear-driven conditions will interrupt this maintenance of peace. This will lead to conditional love, as it eventually lessens the love-growing roots of resistance and leads to a path that will require dealing with shame, guilt, apathy, grief, fear, desire, anger, pride, and finally reaching courage, allowing us a chance for recovery.

There are three magic sentences that, once repeated, will end any internal or external struggle. They will bring peace to any occasion that requires maintenance of peace. They will bring healing to any distress. They will free from one the need to forgive or be forgiven. They will sooth any hurt feelings. They will allow one to recognize and celebrate the connection of all in lieu of being threatened by separations. They will bring comfort to any anxiety and will neutralize any case of depression. They will bring understanding to any misunderstanding. They will fill the void of inadequacy. They will bring an abundance of goodness to all feelings of not being good enough. They bring ecstasy to one's state of turmoil.

However, the magic comes with criteria that will need to be agreed upon in advance, otherwise it will possess no magic and will only be empty words with no effects. This criteria requires a self-imposed agreement between the recipient and him or herself upon receipt of the three sentences. They will need to be repeated frequently for at least three days in response to any of the aforementioned occasions.

The three magic sentences are the following, which must be repeated in the full format each time:

- I am love!
- I am loving!
- And I am beyond that!

In order to be the observer of our experiences and define it as love or hate toward ourselves first and then others, we must understand the dynamics of judgment.

Love flows when we see beauty in both a bush and a flower. Each beauty may have a different shape and form, but they equally and fundamentally have the same beauty and appreciation for their existence and their creation. Hate is consummated when a hierarchical grading system is created to evaluate the two.

"Who judges whom?" And is it possible to judge someone else without experiencing that judgment against ourselves first?

The main reason to judge someone is to satisfy that personal need of wanting to feel better at that moment.

And if we already feel good, then there will be no need to judge anyone to begin with.

How is it that two people meeting a new person have two different views? One says, "How quiet he was," while the other one says, "Did you see how rude he was to be quiet?" Or it's the opposite, where one says, "Did you see how friendly she was?" while the other one says, "She was a fake." Where do we get these opposing views? Marcel Proust said, "The real voyage of discovery consists not in seeking new lands but seeing with new eyes."

The flow of universal energy may be compared with river rafting. The flow is always down from the universe. When we are flowing in this downstream direction, our experiences are of peace, love, joy, and compassion. In a way, we might say that when we go downstream, we are looking at the universe from the same exact angle and view that our creator had intended and is doing. When we go upstream, the experiences are of resistance, dis-ease, anger, and of something less than well-being. In a way, we are looking at the same thing as our creator is, but from a different view.

Somehow as we grow up, something internally shifts us away from looking down the same telescope as our architect. The Dali Lama said, "People take different roads seeking fulfilment and happiness. Just because they're not on your road does not mean that they are lost."

Our misalignment may be summarized as being:

1. Our view is the same as the universe's when we have no desire to be superior or inferior at birth. That is why babies are so lovable, because they remind us of what we have forgotten to be and we ache to regain that original essence.

2. Behavior learned through false teachings and attitudes from the vibration of others, lovingly or otherwise, especially during our childhood, will be one of the main diversions.

3. As the observer having these experiences, we engage in this constant evaluation of others to make us less or more of what we believe to be ourselves in order to feel better.

If the evaluation is less, we feel inferior, and if the evaluation is more, we feel superior. Oscillation between these two polarities is exhausting, and our interpretation of its existence is anger, lying, and deception fighting in opposition to peace, love, and joy, where neutrality resides.

Since we must recognize that "something" within ourselves first before we can determine how to compare with it, then it's impossible not to judge ourselves first. Or, otherwise our neutrality would not have detected such a judgment.

In a way, we can say all judgments are self to self!

Mother Teresa said, "If you judge people, you have no time to love them."

So, what can be learned from this new understanding in order to start a new beginning?

The following quote resonates within us as we celebrate the old and welcome the new change. "The past is history, future is mystery, and NOW is where peace is. That is why it is called present—because it is a gift." Indeed, our power is at now, where peace, love, and joy exist to be our gift which is accessible to all that are accepting it."

When we review our past experiences and dare to fearlessly look at them with open hearts and compassion through the same eyes that we were created by, we indeed see that at every ending there is a new beginning. Every ending gave us new wings to soar to new heights, and without them it would have been impossible to reach those new goals. We recognize that we never arrive, since happiness and joy are the end results of this journey we call life.

Once we realize that the future comes exactly as what we want it to be, we become thrilled about the promise of the future and all impending wellness that the universe has in store for us. We recognize that it is our universal default to be one with that energy that flows, to be at ease and not at dis-ease. We begin to dance to the music of the universe even when our physical eyes and ears assure us with certainty that none is playing.

When we recognize that each ending is only a parenthesis of that one experience before another one starts, we learn to cherish each experience. We find comfort in knowing that we came from nowhere, we are now here, and we go back to nowhere—but not at the same dot that began us, with something different and in a way wiser.

This will pose a new attitude toward welcoming all changes, allowing us to grow as all new year's resolutions transform to "why wait, start now!"

Most of us believe that change comes when the desire to do something different is greater than the discomfort of continuing with what does not seem to be at ease. However, real change comes when the joy of creating what you desire magnifies your attraction to it with such an ease and pleasure that no other avenues can possibly be entertained.

Gandhi said, "We but mirror the world. All the tendencies present in the outer world are to be found in the world of our body. If we could change ourselves, the tendencies in the world would also change. As a man changes his own nature, so does the attitude of the world change towards him. This is the divine mystery supreme. A wonderful thing it is and the source of our happiness. We need not wait to see what others do."

"Be the change that you want to see in the world."

Love and hate are self-generated because if you squeeze an orange, only orange juice would come out. Apple juice will never come out of an orange. So, when they squeeze you, what will come out? Joy, love, and peace, or the opposite: unhappiness, hate, and hostility?

A lot of times we are confused by this and justify our actions by making others or other events responsible as we blame them. If they had behaved in a certain way that was more pleasing to us, then joy, love, and peace would have come out instead of the opposite. However, the truth is that only what is inside can come out.

So where did it all start? If we were all born with only this essence of goodness, then when did the bad and opposite start?

There are many philosophies about the origin of bad. The best explanation may lie in understanding the ego. When you go to bed, you must give up your ego in order to fall asleep, and when you wake up in the morning, it is your ego that demands you get up and attend to the body. Its demands can be as simple as "get up and feed me" or as complicated as "you are so-and-so, get up and conquer the world, and do whatever it takes to accomplish that because I want more."

The book of Genesis from the Old Testament may have one of the explanations. Apparently, the bad started when Adam and Eve's sons had a dispute, and Cain killed Able. Supposedly, Cain and Able were bringing the land's best offering to God as a form of appreciation before eating them. Able, without hesitation, had gathered the best product of what he had harvested, and God had blessed it. Cain had brought his best product too, but hesitated to offer it and questioned offering it, thinking that if he offers less to God, there will be more for himself. God was aware of his thoughts and rejected his offering by not blessing it. Cain became angry and jealous of his brother, and killed him through his unhappiness, hate, and hostility.

Regardless of our religious beliefs or the source we may choose to search for the beginning of bad, the concept presented makes perfect sense. When we understand the unity of all and feel no separation, the absolute result of that internal thought of unity without any resistance is joy, love, and peace. When we have a thought of separation and wanting more for ourselves and less for others, something changes within us that produces something opposite to our true essence, which we interpret as unhappiness, hate, and hostility.

When we believe that the source of our beating heart is limitless and will not diminish, we give without condition and feel no loss. However, when we believe that this source has limitations and diminishes every time we give something away, we become possessive and all forms of giving are considered losses.

The choice is ours: Either we recognize our true essence and align ourselves with the energy that beats our hearts and experience joy, love, and peace, or else we look for a reason for separation and experience the opposite.

CHAPTER SIX

YOU ARE THE CAUSE, NOT THE EFFECT

All the darkness in the world cannot stop the light of a single candle. Be the one who glows. Recognizing that you have to take responsibility for yourself regardless of what the cause may have been gives you power and allows you to take all necessary actions without awaiting others' approval.

This is consistent with the attitude behind all forms of creation:

- God said, "Let there be light," and there was light. This demonstrates an attitude that has no confusion about its ability to create, and it recognizes that all is available and all is well, and once the flow of its energy is allowed, it will flow to transform.

- Saint Francis of Assisi said, "God make me an instrument of thy peace." This demonstrates an attitude that peace is already present but may not have arrived at this location and at this time, but allow me to be the instrument that makes it present at this location and at this time.

- Gandhi said, "Be the change that you want to see in the world." This demonstrates an attitude that positive change already exists. When you make the choice to have it, the surrounding environment will soon reflect that change regardless of current conditions.

To be the cause requires the power stemmed from the intention. But what is intention and where does it come from?

We have all experienced at least one magical moment in our lives where it seems that all obstructions cease to exist and it is impossible not to reach what is desired. Like the moment the basketball, the hoop, and the player all are in perfect alignment, and the distance to the hoop, our physical sight, the blocking defenders, and the conditions of the field no longer have any importance to making the perfect score. It seems that we are magnetically drawn to that goal and, like a bulldog with a tire, it's impossible to give it up.

That magical moment is our first taste of the power of intention. Intention is when all that we know as being us, and all the power that we question (whether we can have it or not), become aligned in harmony to accomplish what is desired. It is that power that no longer allows excuses to be justified nor heard, and whatever has been intended must triumph.

True intentions create whatever action may be necessary to materialize things. In a way, our reality reflects our intentions. Intention comes from so deep within that its purity and wholesomeness can only be questioned by the soul.

When the intention is aligned with all that we believe to be us, it manifests, and when this alignment is not present, we fail to accomplish it.

We are born with clarity to intend and materialize, and somehow we become derailed from that path by maturing to live more by habits and less by intentions. When we flirt with an idea, we usually give attention to it without having any intention to yield any results. When we intend to accomplish something, we focus our attention to produce satisfactory results.

How can we detect lack of alignment of all that is needed to ensure success and practice refinement of our intentions?

Since intention requires action to implement it, detecting confusion about our intention and commitment to its execution must be required and evaluated in order to accomplish it, before the intention has been set.

"By banishing doubt and trusting your intuitive feeling, you clear a space for the power of intention to flow through."
— WAYNE DYER

Clarity about our intention stems from the following self-evaluations as its prerequisites:

- What is my expectation and priority about this intent and what needs do I have?

- What will be required from me to pay my most attention to and what will be missed from my attention since my intention will require me to be consumed with this main focus for proper implementation as my priority?

- What is important to me that will be considered to be a positive move in order for my intention to be carried out? (For example, if I intend to keep a relationship alive, then proving the other person to be wrong over a distressed point may no longer be the priority.)

Every intention will manifest exactly as planned only when attention and focus are in harmony with determination.

So, does it matter what we think in order to implement our intentions?

We think, and because the manifestation is not instant, we believe that our thought did not matter since we could not detect this initial spark that starts the fire. This continues many times over, and eventually we believe that our thoughts are separate from our materialistic experiences due to the time delay that we have become accustomed to.

So, we start having many negative thoughts while awaiting a positive outcome at the end of the day, not realizing that they are related. If you wonder why you are experiencing this now, investigate what you were thinking before; and if you wonder what you will be experiencing in the future, investigate what you are thinking now.

Our thoughts provide direction exactly same as an arrow needing a sharp tip to accurately find its way to the target. Joyfulness and depression require an equal amount of energy in order to provide their positive or negative outcome. The only difference between the two is their direction. In a way we can say depression is the same energy as joyfulness that has gone backward. If what we think matters and materializes, then why is there a time delay? Why isn't there instant manifestation?

The answer lies in the perfection of the universe and our creator, that all is well and accounted for and nothing is missing. The only missing part is our lack of understanding as the observer at the time that we think something is missing.

Imagine that you're learning how to drive a car. Would it be safe to allow you to drive a racing car driving at two hundred fifty miles per hour when a novice speed should only be fifty miles per hour? Of course not, you would not be able to react safely and would hurt yourself and others. In the same way, imagine that you have not learned and mastered that the only language of universe is love, peace, and compassion. What if you get mad at someone and with instant manifestation power you say, "I hope that your leg breaks" and immediately their leg is broken?

Amazingly, we notice that as our intention becomes clearer and our thoughts remain pure and in line with the universal flow, when we only wish well for ourselves and others, when we trust that universe's default is always well, when we have compassion and love for all beings and always seek peace, the timing for manifestation of all our desires becomes exponentially faster.

Maharishi Effect meditation study research has shown that when a group of people focus and meditate on peace with the same intention around the world, the world around us responds favorably and events change. When you are in love, the world seems loving; when you are in turmoil, everyone looks like an enemy, and soon the outer world will transform to match those inner thoughts.

Therefore, thought management is no longer an option or a personal preference, but a responsibility to ourselves first and the universe as a whole.

So, if our thoughts and their management are important, then what should we be looking for in order to have a direction?

Most of us use all our resources to find the right outfit, shoes, car, food, vacation spot, house, and all our materialistic needs. Knowingly or unknowingly, we do the same with all our relationships. We search for that companion or friend or business relationship by giving attention to the ones who meet that hidden criteria that we had set up in our mind. By this process of knowingly or unknowingly including or excluding, we connect with all that finally comes to our experiences.

Every time that our attention is given to something desired or undesired, an energetic field is created around us that will attract or repel other magnetic fields in the universe. In a way, there is no accident when two cars collide in the middle of an intersection when the other ten cars pass each other without the desire to attract. We tend to personalize our negative events to find comfort by blaming ourselves, someone, or something outside, in search for a reason for why undesired things happen.

However, the universe does not understand blame other than different polarities of energy. This means that the universe, without any personal agenda, may send us to a hospital to relax instead of a sunny vacation day at the beach when we ask for a break but are not clear in our asking.

Thoughts by themselves remain in energetic field of thoughts. However, thoughts leading to materialistic experiences require the power of emotions to become a reality that can be comprehended by our feelings and senses. These experiences are the only things that we find important to us individually, since our comprehension of them makes them our truth. Is there a sound of wind in the forest if there is no ear to hear it? The happiness, sorrow, or neutrality that exists in the world only becomes your truth when you become aware of it and internally process it to some form of feeling.

Consequently, what we look for and what we find determines our reality as co-creations, somehow related in energetic forces and in lieu of the myth of their independency. This energetic entanglement is independent from any interpretation of personal blame due to the outcome of what may or may not be desired.

An old Cherokee is teaching his grandson about life. "A fight is going on inside me," he said to the boy. "It is a terrible fight and it is between two wolves. One is evil – he is anger, envy, sorrow, regret, greed, arrogance, self-pity, guilt, resentment, inferiority, lies, false pride, superiority, and ego." He continued, "The other is good – he is joy, peace, love, hope, serenity, humility, kindness, benevolence, empathy, generosity, truth, compassion, and faith. The same fight is going on inside you – and inside every other person, too."

The grandson thought about it for a minute and then asked his grandfather, "Which wolf will win?". The old Cherokee simply replied, "The one you feed more."

We always find what we are looking for. When we look for prosperity, we find it. When we look for its lack, we find that too. When we look for health, we find it. When we look for a disease, it will present itself. When we look for struggle, we find it. When we look for peace, all opportunities to be peaceful arise. When we look for happiness, all the reasons to be happy show up. When we look for unhappiness, there are no justifications and reasons seem to be adequate to be anything different.

———

Indeed, when we look for good things, we find them, and when we worry about the bad by looking into it, we find that too. However, when we dissect the bad, we realize that bad is defined as the things that we want to be missing from our experiences. A person who qualifies disease as bad is only missing the ease and pleasure of perfect health.

All relationships are much better at the beginning. The main reason is that both parties look for the things they want to see in each other in the beginning. They look for good things and they find them, rather than looking for lacks and missing things that later they seek, but they end up finding those too as the relationship changes.

So, what are you looking for? The teacher and the lesson are always available; however, the lesson is only learned when the student is ready to absorb it and looks for it. Once we realize that thoughts become things, we carefully manage our thoughts to direct ourselves to what we want by giving all the attention to what is desired and eliminating all energy toward what is undesired.

But what if our focus is on inadequacy?

Whatever we focus on becomes our reality! When our focus is on lack of something, the lack will continue appearing in our experiences until we finally get tired of those experiences and realize that this universe is a giving and doing universe and will not understand the lack.

A lot of us may intend to focus on having something that is more pleasing to us, but somehow it appears that there is an internal confusion between what we intend to do versus what we energetically emit. Like a magnet, we consciously or unconsciously polarize the events to come to us or to be distracted from us.

Thoughts become things based on our path of least resistance. The best way to redirect your thoughts away from something that you do not desire is to give it no attention at all. Redirect your thoughts toward what you desire every time that your focus gets pointed to the lack. Reinforce your thoughts consciously and repeatedly toward what you desire as much as possible until that becomes your new path of least resistance.

You were disciplined enough to focus on the lack, so the good news is that you know you have the discipline to redirect yourself toward something equal but in the opposite direction.

It reminds me of this quote: "If you wonder why you are experiencing this now, investigate what you were thinking before. If you wonder what you will be experiencing in the future, investigate what you are thinking now."

Accordingly, understanding and gaining this knowledge is the most valuable, but when will change come?

Change comes when our focus and attention shift from what is to what is desired. Our thoughts are a form of pure invisible energy that constantly creates experiences through our brain's neurotransmitters, nervous system, chemical reactions, and biological changes, and that has end results in the form of our emotions and feelings. This appears to be a one-way communication at first, but it is not.

Very quickly, these previous emotional experiences impact our future thoughts and desires. Eventually, we become our environment and allow it to control our desires. The body dictates the thoughts we should have based on emotions and previous experiences, as opposed to our thoughts having unlimited energetic power of imagination that allows us to soar to the sky with many possibilities.

Change requires wanting to have experiences greater than our environment. This requires a burst of energy in excess of our comfortable norm. This uncomfortable feeling of transition is usually what stops us from making change. Fear of the unknown and discomfort blocks our potential for growth and expansion.

Change is good and enjoyable when directed by our joyful desires. In contrast, sometimes we look for change due to our confusion, not realizing that we look to change because of running away from something undesired. That change is temporary since we eventually get tired of constantly changing in search of a relief. There is no amount of changing that will substitute the reasons for our running away.

Sometimes we want everyone else to change so we can feel better about ourselves. We become pessimistic and constant complainers, since we see the glass as always being half empty. Because we are always controlled by others' behaviors, we will never find comfort in this method of change. Rumi said, "Yesterday I was clever, so I wanted to change the world. Today I am wise, so I am changing myself."

At times, the universe will force us to change. Circumstances make us redirect from the road that we are travelling leading to destruction to a new path leading to bliss. Many times, we do not understand this blessing and confuse that with a curse, but eventually our faith in the wisdom of universe guides us through.

"When the world pushes you to your knees, you
are in a perfect position to pray." — RUMI

Joe Dispenza's *Breaking the Habit of Being Yourself* is a valuable resource describing our psyche that offers many tools that can be used to make change. It says that the path to change is relearning, reinventing a new self, sprouting new connections, reconditioning the body for a new mind or emotion, creating a new one, becoming familiar with the new self, reprogramming, creating a new future, and finally developing a new energy.

The good news is that joyfulness and misery are two opposite extremes of our beings requiring the same amount of energy. This means that if you have the capability to be miserable, then you have already proven that you have the capability to be joyful through a simple redirection of your thoughts and consciously choosing to make a change for your new personality, which becomes your new personal reality.

Rumi said, "Try not to resist the changes that come your way. Instead let life live through you. And do not worry that your life is turning upside down. How do you know that the side you are used to is better than the one to come?"

With this new knowledge, how can we ensure that change comes for better, directing us toward what is desired? The simple answer would be to anticipate good things!

Entertain yourself with this simple exercise to see who you truly are on the inside and how you view the world.

Take a few minutes to quiet your mind and walk outside, away from disturbances. Look at a tree or a flower from a few feet away. Just observe quietly. Now, continue looking at the same thing, but start anticipating that something good is happening. There's no need to be specific about what it is, just anticipate that something good is going to happen and keep that thought for a while by quietly repeating it in your mind.

After a while you will notice an amazing transformation. Most people will notice that their vision expands, their head opens up, their body relaxes, the depth and beauty of what they were looking at magnifies, they notice more details that were not apparent before, they feel joy and appreciation for their state of being that was not there before—the foggy glasses used to look at life get replaced with crystal-clear clarity and beauty that was unnoticed before. They will no longer notice the difference between a bush or a flower, only beauty, calmness, appreciation for this state of being, and this experience of being present now.

This is the state that we were created to be in at all times. A state of bliss. The comfort of knowing that all is well. That the universe's default is always good. The state of being where we can manifest all that is desired, since there is no resistance, just going down the river with the flow. This is the state of ease that dis-ease cannot exist in.

At this state, we realize that we are spiritual beings having physical experiences and not physical beings tired of all the daily stresses who reach to anything that will give us relief by forgetting how fearful and stressful we are at every moment of our lives. This is the state of Zen, where we become citizens of the present and are no longer hostages of our pasts, nor chained by the fear of future.

It reminds me of this story: A yogi was sitting quietly in a corner, meditating and smiling. The villagers came and complained to him, questioning how he could possibly be sitting in this corner meditating and smiling and at such peace with all the famine, war, hate, poverty, filth, and struggle. He said, "In my world, nothing ever goes wrong." Imagine such power and confidence to be able to act independent from the opinion of others. To be the one who dares to view the world from the same angle that our creator does. Indeed, that is the moment when the promise of that future comes, when we believe that it will come just the way we want it.

Once we realize that there is no amount of exploring sickness that will bring health, no amount of focusing on poverty that will bring prosperity, no amount of strategizing anti-war methods that will bring peace, and no amount of resisting fear that will allow us to be loving, we realize that the promise of future must come when we anticipate good things happening. The wellness comes when we are thrilled about its pending. The prosperity comes when we allow it to attract that polarity before seeing its physical evidence.

"The beauty you see in me is a reflection of you." — RUMI

The future comes exactly the way that the promise of future is anticipated. Anticipate good things!

So, how can we ensure that our intentions, thoughts, and desired courses of action from all the above remain uncontaminated from the opinions of others?

We all receive many opinions from others about how we should live our lives and the kind of decisions that we should be making every day. Some are good, uplifting and encouraging. Some are offered with good intentions but do not fit well with the goals and agendas that we have for our lives. And some are provided with negative, narrow-minded points of views and, in some cases, are destructive, coming from the point of lack, scarcity, and jealousy of the providers.

Dr. Seuss gave us the simple answer when we were kids, but somehow we forgot it as we grew up: "Those who matter don't mind, and those who mind don't matter" (originally quoted by B. Baruch).

Milk others' opinions when provided positively, and allow them to be the wind under your wings if you choose to apply them. Examine other opinions that may be good advice but not applicable to your life and goals, and choose wisely, knowing that the choice is yours.

Finally, do not give attention to the negative opinion of others, since it generally comes from their personal view of lack and fear independent from what may be applicable to you. Not giving attention and not allowing that opinion to disturb us may be more difficult at times, because most of us have not developed the strength that acting independently from opinion of others may require.

Why is it that the things others say or do still bother us? Well, the answer may be simple. You cannot give away something that you do not have. In a way, it is impossible to react to something if it does not have anything internally that can positively or negatively harmonize with it to trigger a reaction. External acts of love to others require internal recognition of love within. External acts of retaliation with physical action or without it, creating internal turmoil, still require some internal recognition, otherwise we will have no reaction other than observation.

When we see an act of love and compassion, we cry because something inside has recognized that similarity that creates the combustion of the overwhelming reaction of crying. Similarly, when we hear a negative comment or someone's opinion, we react only when there is something inside triggering that doubt.

Here is a simple clearing method that may be useful in clearing your mind from others' negative opinions and your self-defeating thoughts. Repeat to yourself when needed: "Take out the trash" (from the book, *Peaceful Warrior*). Then, imagine that you are actually removing that thought like trash and throwing it away. Try to physically detach from it as you send it out of your mind to be carried away and eventually burned in a faraway incinerator.

Our freedom and individual development and growth starts when we learn and are satisfied to enjoy life by accomplishing our goals liberated from the judgment of others. Once we shift our focus from opinion of others to our self-development, we see beauty in everything independent from the distortion offered by others and stemmed from their insecurities.

> "Be independent of the good opinion of other people."
> — A. MASLOW

We are habitual beings and develop patterns that may or may not be desirable. In order to accomplish all the above, we must be open to breaking the chain of pattern and be willing to act at will once their unsatisfactory formation has been detected.

If you observe those around you and your own life stories, you will quickly notice a certain pattern that repeats itself regardless of the participating elements. It can be personal relationships, business dealings, affectionate affairs, struggle situations, or any other form of transaction. The common link always remains to be the individual having that pattern.

The ones who are peaceful are always involved with peaceful activities. The ones who are in struggle remain in struggle, regardless of where they are and whom they associate with, and the pattern continues until the one with the common link decides to break it. The ones who are appreciative of family, friends, colleagues, and neighbors remain appreciative, and the ones who are not continue to not recognize that.

Scientists and mathematicians have shown that there is a repetitive pattern of creation that duplicates itself until the space that is allocated to it is filled or something drastic happens to change it. A snowflake that is broken down to the smallest segment shows that it is a triangle repeating itself over and over again. The tree, the flowers, the human cells, the DNA, the cosmic organization and pattern of galaxies all follow a certain repetitive pattern.

This pattern has been calculated to have a formula defined as $Z = Z^2 + C$, with Z being the input and C being a common factor. Once Z and C are established at conception of the pattern, they keep repeating themselves and escalating, as the new input Z becomes the old output of what was used before. This keeps repeating until something is changed or the space that they occupy is saturated.

What does this mean as far as our human behavior, and how does it apply to our daily lives? The most important question would be, how can we benefit from this knowledge and break the chain of undesired patterns?

The cyclical pattern that is experienced in each circumstance has a common element of a certain behavior linked to the person experiencing it. Also, this means that the constant repetitive common element must be changed if the pattern is undesirable and is to be broken and replaced with a new preferred pattern.

Basically, if C is a lack of abundance, then the cycle will always show lack of prosperity regardless of transaction and favorable or unfavorable odds. If C is love, that repeats itself many times over as the pattern continues. If C is not being good enough, the cycle will repeat and will include that factor in all the transactions.

Change comes when we act above our environment and act beyond what is considered to be our norm. In order to make a conscious change, we must clearly define the pattern and clearly intend to change it by doing the following. Each time the pattern C factor appears, immediately state in your mind CHANGE and replace it with your new desired C factor.

"The secret of change is to focus all of your energy not on fighting the old, but on building the new." — SOCRATES

With all this knowledge, how can we be assured that we really get it, and when will that recognition truly be present, comparing to all those other times that we had thought we got it?

Have you ever pondered about something over and over again? Then you think *I really got it*, but you keep pondering on it because you're not satisfied with the closure. Finally, one day, unplanned and unexpected, the answer presents itself, the search ends, and the desire to seek for more ceases. It feels as you really got it this time.

If you have ever experienced this, you become like a small child again, wanting to jump up and down with joy as you have finally received the toy that you have been waiting for months or years.

Many of us are confused and puzzled by our purpose in life. Our purposes are those quiet voices within that gently whisper to us without closure until we *really* get it.

A lot of us become impatient, sad, and depressed, and we do not enjoy the journey along this path, since we only find satisfaction when we reach the destination, not recognizing that the search for purpose is part of the process.

"Getting it" or "not getting it" are both equally valued with no hierarchy of ego-driven opinions, since they are simply the state of "it is". "It is" is a state where we are flowing in the universal downstream direction in joy and peace. You become the observer to enjoy the ride in lieu of struggling to swim upstream. At this state, you are inspired to live experiencing the infinite possibilities of your energetic being in physical materialistic form. At this state, we really get it, since we see equal beauty in both the bush and the flower, in absence of judgment.

When the focus is on the prize stemmed from the ego and is fed pending the satisfaction of others, we think that we "get it," but it seems that we are still searching for closure. It seems that we can only explore our full capabilities but with many limitations. However, when we "*really* get it," it seems that we finally explore our infinite possibilities, we are satisfied with whatever it is, and we no longer search for closure. The observer who decides to search is satisfied with perfection at that stage.

Allow your infinite being to explore this limited physical experience of one hundred years, not from this small window of one hundred years, but from the door that had allowed you to enter this experience from the timeless being that you truly are in order to *really* get it. Allow the universal essence of joy, peace, love, and compassion to be the door and the torch that will light your way so there will be no path other than "*really* getting it."

"What lies behind us and what lies ahead of us are tiny matters compared to what lies within us." — RALPH W. EMERSON

There is a magical secret that makes it all possible, and that is the magic of willingness!

If you are truthful about observing your life and all those times that you immediately acted or unknowingly held back, you will be surprised to find out how your willingness had impacted the outcome of everything you had experienced.

Children and teenagers are masters of demonstrating what willingness is and how it works. When they want something and are willing to accomplish it, it is done faster than the speed of light. However, if it is something that they are not willing to do, all the simplest reasons in the world block them. The sun is not round enough, the moon is not bright enough, the temperature is not cool enough, the sky is not blue enough, and more.

This was harshly demonstrated in one of the best movies of our time, *Schindler's List*. Mr. Schindler purchases a factory that makes bolts for fighter jets during World War II in Nazi Germany. The goal is to save Jews from concentration camps by having them work at this factory with the intent of not supporting the war and building nothing through low production of bolts—just enough to not get caught. Mr. Schindler bribes the inspectors as much as he can in order not to be noticed. One day, there is a surprise inspection by a new Nazi commander. He walks around the production facility, getting a tour as he observes all the Jewish prisoners who appear to be working hard. He stops at one of the stations and questions the operator curiously, asking him to demonstrate his job. The operator nervously and speedily makes a new bolt to impress the inspector. The prisoner, assuming that he is showing how productive he can be, does it as fast as possible, in less than a minute. The inspector looks at the bolt and then looks at the box of his production collection and realizes that the operator can produce at the rate of one per minute when he has been producing at the rate of one per hour all morning. The inspector kills him on the spot.

What is the cause of this unseen, unspoken magic of willingness that when we have it, we move at the speed of light, and when we do not, we move slower than a turtle toward whatever the goal may be? What can we do to consciously promote willingness to accomplish more of the things that we desire in a joyful way?

"Inspired" is one of my favorite words. It comes from being in spirit. We define spirit as being limitless, unbound by friction of the body, capable of traveling at the speed of light. When we are inspired, we feel no friction, we fly to any elevation without hesitation. In a way, willingness is stemmed from being inspired. Find a way to be inspired about whatever desire that you may have, and you will find yourself willing to make it happen under all circumstances regardless of conditions. Willingness is the first step from neutrality to give us direction toward what is desired. Willingness is supposed to be the first step toward the path to joy and peace beyond neutrality. In the hierarchy of the vibrational path to joy and peace, reason allows acceptance to advance, and acceptance upholds willingness.

> "Pure love is a willingness to give without a thought of receiving anything in return." — PEACE PILGRIM

Ah, at last, we realize that we are the cause and not the effect, as we finally have the first glimpse of true happiness!

I recall that my son, at the age of ten, showed us a quote that he had written on his window; he had clouded it so it would stand out. I had never before witnessed the first glimpse of recognition of anyone's true power for happiness. It was amazing to see that this young ten-year-old boy had discovered this simple truth about his reality when many of us die without recognizing that. It is so simple, and yet it seems distant from many of us.

Our absolute true power lies in our ability to decide. Once we recognize that each decision directs us to a different path and our only task is to make a decision and then enjoy the ride, at that moment we have had the first glimpse of recognizing our true power.

It is not the difficulty of the path nor the obstacles along the way that make our goals unachievable. It is the recognition of the power that goes with realizing that once we make a decision and maintain it with a single thought of determination, that makes every goal achievable.

It is impossible for the universe not to deliver what you have decided on when it is truly being focused on. When it is made with happiness, compassion, and thinking of the unity of all, the energetic path of the sun, the moon, the stars, and the universe align themselves to assist you in accomplishing it. When it is contradictory to the above, all those forces provide many reasons for why it should not have been done. Any emotion other than happiness may be considered contradictory to the forces of universe, since the universe flows at ease and our interpretation of forces opposing it are dis-ease.

The dying old man gave his last advice to his family and said, "I have seen many troubles in my life, but most of them never happened." How is it that some people see trouble while other people looking at the same circumstances see just another opportunity to grow and move in a different direction? When we choose to change how we look at things, things do indeed change. When we choose to see happiness regardless of conditions, we find happiness all around us, and when we choose to find sorrow, there is no place where we can be without experiencing sorrow.

Einstein said, "The most important decision we make is whether we believe we live in a friendly or hostile universe." From that moment on, everything will change relative to that decision. When we see the world as friendly, we no longer dismiss the bush for what it looks like and find no reason to praise the flower for its beauty. You only see creation at its perfection and appreciate the grace that made it all possible.

I read the quote on my son's window one more time before I went to bed that night, and reminded myself of it so I would never forget that first glimpse of realizng the power to be happy, which I had fogotten as I grew up. It said:

"People are just as happy as they make up their minds to be."
— ABRAHAM LINCOLN

CHAPTER SEVEN

SILENCE, KNOWLEDGE, FEAR, DOUBT, AND AT LAST, FREEDOM

W hen Michelangelo was praised for his masterpiece statue *David*, he simply responded, "I saw David in the stone and set him free by carving the extra pieces away." What do you see in a piece of stone? What do you see with your eyes closed? And what do you see when you are free from all your thoughts? What do you see as the end product of any new desire and task that you have?

It seems that as we grow up, all of us knowingly or unknowingly build armor around ourselves to protect against all our fears and disappointments and further threats. Very soon we forget about enjoying life and become preoccupied with tending the armor to make sure it is ready to protect us at all times.

The Knight in Rusty Armor by Robert Fisher tells a story that is conclusive of it all. He masterfully walks us through the life of a knight lost in his purpose to live, not knowing why or what he is living for.

The story begins with a knight who was the greatest in the kingdom and the king's favorite. Always ready to march to any threat facing the kingdom, he had shiny armor with all his gear and his horse ready for action. He spent all his day polishing the armor, sharpening his sword, and tending to his horse, to make sure that he was always the best of the best. He was proud that as he walked through the city, the sun radiated from his armor and he could hear the praise of all the kingdom for how great he was.

He grew older, got married, had a son, and lived in his castle near the king. There was peace all over the kingdom, and there were no more threats, so there was no more use for the knight's services. But he always had his armor on, since he had gotten used to it, and was always ready to protect and had no time for his family. Eventually time passed, and because he had not used his armor, his armor started to rust to the point that he could not move anymore. His helmet would not open to allow him to eat. He could not take off his armor, and very soon he became the prisoner of his own armor.

He realized that he would die if he did not find a way to take off his armor. He reached out to the king, who was his friend, and king told him the only person who could help him was the wizard who lived deep in the middle of the jungle. So, the knight said goodbye to his wife and his son and headed to the jungle.

After many beautiful events, he found the wizard, who agreed to help him and assigned two of his assistants to help him—a squirrel, who used his small hands to feed the knight through his helmet , and Rebecca the bird, who flew over the knight's head to show him the way.

At first the knight had no respect for the two animals, since he thought humans were superior to animals, but very soon they became friends. As three of them talked to each other more, he realized that they were his only hope for survival and much wiser than him.

The wizard had told the knight that in order to take off his armor, he had to conquer and pass through the three castles, and that this did not require any of his fighting skills. The first castle was the Castle of Silence, the second was Knowledge, and the third was the castle of Will and Daring.

As he passed through each of these castles with beautiful terms of events and enlightenments, each piece of his armor fell apart. After he passed through the last castle, the only armor left was his breast plate. He found himself at top of the cliff with the last riddle to solve, which tells him to let go of the cliff that he is hanging on to for dear life. It said that "if you let go, you will not drop down into the bottom of the abyss, but you will be elevated to the top of the mountain instead."

"Though this universe I own, I possess not a thing, for I cannot know the unknown if to the known I cling." He finally trusted and let go of all fear, and allowed himself to fall into the abyss. To his surprise, the breast plate came off and he rose up to the top of the mountain instead, finding his path back home to his family as a new man. "For indeed, the knight was the brook. He was the moon. He was the sun. He could be all those things at once now, and more, because he was one with the universe. He was love" (quoted from the book's final chapter).

Each of us, with whatever personal stories that we may have, when seeking to hear our voice within, must travel through the same castles, forming our own experiences and guiding us to that forgotten voice.

The Castle of Silence

Many of us run aggressively toward our goals. We make many sacrifices. We accept no excuses. We accomplish what is needed to get to that goal and run faster and faster at all costs, and we take pride in how fast we run. It is undisputable that setting and accomplishing goals are pleasurable experiences; however, when this running is no longer joyful and is stressful, then we need to stop and ask, are we running toward a desired goal or are we running away from something that is undesirable, something that we fear will destroy us if we stop to face it?

Running away may be to avoid something or to forget about a tragedy, or it simply may be not having found meaning in our daily life. Regardless of what makes us run, it misleads us by changing our attention toward a temporary solution. We eventually accomplish that goal and, since it was not the right reason to begin with, we find ourselves needing to run again by finding another excuse and a new target as a new goal without enjoyment. This eventually stops as we become so exhausted in this unpleasant experience that we can no longer continue, and we look for a true target that makes us joyful unconditionally.

How can we detect this so we can redirect our path?

When you can be silent and have no need to run away from anything, you recognize the beauty and pleasure of wanting to freely run toward something that you truly desire. Listen to the sound of silence; it has a music that is indescribable. It has the answer to all the questions. It is the absolute solution because once it is divided, it is still silence and it will never diminish.

> *"In the attitude of silence, the soul finds the path in a clearer light, and what is elusive and deceptive resolve itself into crystal clearness. Our life is a long and arduous quest after truth."*
> — MAHATMA GANDHI

How do we find silence when we have been trained to always do something and be busy?

The best practice is to have deliberate periods of daily mental fasting by quieting down our brain and not allowing it to have any thoughts, regardless of how positive or negative they may be. This can be done sitting down comfortably in meditation or in any position at any time.

Another method of energy clearing is to close your eyes and imagine a white light behind you. The white light projects through you from behind and shines through your entire body, clearing your body of any discomfort. Scan the light behind you up and down your body, from the top down. Eventually focus at your head level and allow it to clear your head of any undesired thoughts as it projects through your head, pushing all thoughts outside your body as they fade away, disappearing in front of you. After a while, it will feel as if your body is a hologram with the white light passing completely through it, leaving no shadows.-(GEMeditation With White Light Therapy by Author)

What if the secret to happiness is much simpler than what we had thought and could be experienced by just following these simple three steps? Upon waking, affirm that this is the best day of your life. During the day, find a short period of silence with no thoughts. Prior to sleeping at night, thank the source that has made it all possible, for the daily experiences that you had, and for all that you had learned. Indeed the beauty of the song bird can only be realized when superimposed over the silence.

The Castle of Knowledge

Einstein said, "Imagination is more important than knowledge." Indeed, it is, because imagination gives us wings to fly where knowledge allows us to run faster. Regardless of how much knowledge you may gain, without imagination you will never be able to lift off the ground to enter a different dimension of your experiences.

Conversely, you need to learn to run as fast as you can to create the momentum needed to fly, so gaining knowledge is a prerequisite for bringing our imaginations to reality.

Knowledge is the light that brings clarity to all confusion. It is the understanding that allows us to solve and clear all misunderstandings. With knowledge, we see the link between all things and see how they are all connected. Without knowledge, we look at oceans, clouds, moisture, condensation, and water as being independent from each other. With knowledge, we realize their links—they all have the same essence of water in different forms, but exist under different temperatures and pressures. They are all capable of becoming the other under different circumstances and phases.

Knowledge changes how we look at things, and different outcomes present themselves.

> *"Change how you look at things and things will change."*
> — WAYNE DYER

Contradictory to the above, knowledge gained under fear will be ignorance and brings confusion and despair in lieu of clarity and understanding. Hitler, as the minister of education, planned his future World War II by feeding young children poisonous knowledge stemmed from his fright and misunderstanding, using educational material in order to serve his selfish objectives. However, with true knowledge leading to love and understanding, we are assured that we always act with compassion, since it removes the dark, foggy lenses from our vision, which is designed to only see love when we choose to look at life from the same exact angle that our creator does.

Knowledge has no specific method or style and can present itself at any time, in any place, and under any circumstances. It flows from any angle and has no boundary and limitation. As long as the student is ready, the knowledge is available to be learned. Khalil Gibran said, "I have learned silence from the talkative, toleration from the intolerant, and kindness from the unkind; yet, strange, I am ungrateful to those teachers."

With knowledge, we realize the connectivity of all beings, and with ignorance, we realize their separation.

"Science knows no country, because knowledge belongs to humanity, and is the torch which illuminates the world." — LOUIS PASTEUR

The Castle of Will and Daring

We usually refer to those who have strong determination and willingness to do whatever it takes, who are brave and daring enough to go to any extent to accomplish what they desire, as being enthusiastic. Enthusiasm comes from the Greek words of; "en" means "in," and the root word "theos" means "God." In a way; "enthusiasm" means "God within."

It appears that once we realize the power and connection to the source that makes our heart beat, we connect to this universal power that makes all hearts beat and makes all things possible. This is accomplished when we cease looking for any reason for our separation and taking personal credit for this power. This may be compared to a drop of ocean that, when separated from its source, it no longer has any power, but once it recognizes its connection to the ocean, it has all the power and can move mountains.

Without being willing and daring, we will never experience anything new to transition and expand to, since the fear of the unknown will hold us back. We may be safe but never recognize our full capabilities. Rumi said, "What strange beings we are! That sitting in hell at the bottom of dark, we are afraid of our own immortality."

The certainty is that we know we ride on the shoulder of a giant, and all we need to do is to learn to whisper in his ears so we can accomplish all that we desire. However, like a little child who is always looking for another toy, we are afraid of the power of being able to have all the toys. If we have all the toys, then where would the challenge be? The only thing left would be the absolute enjoyment of joy, love, peace, and compassion that is present in nature, animals, and humans and that we call bliss. It scares us to be at bliss because of the wrong conditioning of all those before us who said there must be hardship, war, sorrow, and pain, so we prepare ourselves to experience those things and they present themselves in all our experiences. We must be willing and daring to stop all wrong conditioning.

Sometimes we are willing and daring to find a transition because we are running away from something, and sometimes our desires make us willing and daring. The first one is exhausting, tiresome, and without enjoyment since we transition looking for relief. Contradictorily, the second one is driven by our desires, and its expansion is joyful and elated. Regardless of how we choose to expand our experiences, we must be satisfied to enjoy the present and to be eager to experience more in the future.

Indeed, the final quest of all our efforts to be willing and daring is when we finally achieve what John Lennon sang about in his masterpiece, "Imagine"—seeing the world through the eyes of the one who created it all:

"Imagine there's no heaven
It's easy if you try
No hell below us
Above us only sky
Imagine all the people living for today
Imagine there's no countries
It isn't hard to do
Nothing to kill or die for
And no religion too
Imagine all the people living life in peace
You may say I'm a dreamer
But I'm not the only one
I hope someday you'll join us

And the world will be as one

Imagine no possessions

I wonder if you can

No need for greed or hunger

A brotherhood of man

Imagine all the people sharing all the world

You may say I'm a dreamer

But I'm not the only one

I hope someday you'll join us

And the world will be as one"

It seems as we all struggle to imagine what John Lennon sang about, as many of us are faced with these three questions on a daily basis:

- What is the right thing to do?
- Who is the most important one?
- When is the right time to do it?

Leo Tolstoy masterfully depicts in his book "The three questions", a king who had asked his nation these questions, promising great rewards for the right answers. Politicians, businessmen, clergymen, educators, physicians, soldiers, and others all offer self-serving answers that displease the king. The king's advisors suggest that the only person with the right answers is the wizard who lives deep in the jungles.

The king, anxious to find the answers, heads to the jungle with his troop. They camp near the jungle and the king, alone in commoner's clothes, goes to find the wizard. He finds him on a warm sunny day digging a large hole near his tent. The king says, "Wizard, I have come looking for the answers to these three questions," and he recites them. The wizard continues digging and finally, after several trials, the wizard says; "Let me finish digging the hole and we will attend to your questions later."

Tired of waiting, the king says to the wizard, "You are an old man digging this large hole on this warm sunny day. Let me help you." The end of the day comes and the hole is finished when the king, tired of waiting and working all day, says, "Wizard, I have been waiting all day and the hole is done. Please give me the answers to these three questions or tell me if you do not know so I can be on my way."

Suddenly, the wizard says, "Be quiet, someone is coming." A man, wounded and bleeding, comes out of the jungle.

The king and wizard run to the man and bring him to the tent. The king nurses him all night until the bleeding stops. Near dawn, the tired king falls asleep next to his patient. When he wakes up, he sees the injured man looking at him, smiling and appreciative of what the king had done. The man says to the king, "You do not know me, but I know you." The king is surprised. The man says, "You had unjustly ordered to execute my brother and to confiscate all his belongings. I had vowed to find and kill you. I knew that you were here alone without your guards. So, I hid in the jungle waiting for you to come back, to ambush you. Finally, when you did not come back, I got tired and came looking for you when your guards blocked me and wounded me. Now, if it was not for you taking care of me, I would have been dead. I am indebted to you and will be at your service from now on."

The king listens to his story and all that was unjustly done to his family. He orders that all that was taken away be given back, and he sends the man back safely to his home.

Then king says, "Wizard, I have been here all day and all night waiting, and you still have not given me the answers to what I had come here for. Please give me the answers so I can be on my way."

The wizard says, "What do you mean? Your questions have already been answered." The king does not understand.

The wizard continues: "When you came here yesterday and saw an old man digging a hole, the most important one was me. The right time was when you decided to help, and the right thing to do was helping me digging the hole.

"When you saw the injured man, the most important one was the injured man; the right time was when you rushed him to my tent to help him, otherwise he would have been dead; and the right thing was for you to nurse him all night to recovery. You see the answers to your questions are very simple: the right time is always now, the most important one is the person you are with, and the right thing to do is always to do good. If you were not delayed by doing good to help me and had left early, the man would have ambushed and killed you."

Indeed, a beautiful story! However, it is your choice to make it a reality by practicing it and challenging others to apply these three questions in their daily lives. Peace can only come when each of us acts in a peaceful manner and does good not for a selected group, and not in special times, but always and under all conditions as the essence of our being.

Through her near-death experience, Anita Moorjani gained the wisdom that what happens to us in this life is a conscious choice of belief. She was given the choice of passing through the energetic wall of death with no option to return and the choice to continue living with the understanding that she can be whatever she wants to be, including her expedited healing from lymphatic cancer. She shared her story with the rest of the world though her book *Dying to Be Me*. Her second book, *What If This Is Heaven?*, is continuation of that understanding and a must-read for all. It is an encouragement for those who do not believe this is heaven and an affirmation for others.

It seems that we have been wrongly trained from very beginning to constantly look for other reasons in the future to make us happy. *Once I get there, I will be truly happy. Once I have that, I will truly be happy. If I can have that romantic partner, I will be truly happy.* . . . Soon we live a life of misery in search of that happiness, and once found, it lasts for a short while before we start searching again. Therefore, true happiness never comes, since we are always waiting for it.

Subsequently, if the concept is wrong, then it will never be satisfying. Like addicts, we constantly look for another fix to find the relief that we have mistakenly learned to associate with happiness.

So, what is the right concept? Through his research (*The Journey of Souls*) of several hundred hypnosis cases, Michael Newton, PhD, documented different people's experiences before they were born and when they had died last. He noticed a similarity among many of the experiences, as if they had an "oops" reaction when they died. *Oops, I confused myself to be my body. Oops, I separated myself from others by borders, races, skin colors, and body shapes. Oops, I thought I was more or less valuable because I valued myself and others by what materialistic things I had collected. Oops. . . . Oops. . . .*

All the oopses mainly stem from our misalignment from our energetic path toward becoming one who only sees beauty in all creation and does not see lack or missing parts in anything. They see only perfection and completeness from the wholeness that creates it all.

If you can read this chapter, then you must have lived several thousand days. For the next seven days, entertain yourself by doing the following two things, and then observe your views of life and your state of being. You will be amazed at how you evaluate everything differently.

1. Each morning when you get up, repeat to yourself: "This is the best day of my life."

2. Then, take a moment and look outside at nature—the sky, the clouds, the sun, the rain, the ocean, the mountain, and your surroundings—and say, "This is heaven." Based on your belief, thank the source that has allowed you to have such an amazing experience in such a beautiful vehicle that can experience all of

this with such perfection. Keep reminding yourself of the above during your day.

Notice how you view all the events of your life that day and take note of how they are different when you do not view the world with this new insight. You will notice that you will have compassion in response to hate, cooperation instead of competitiveness, forgiveness in response to injury, faith in response to doubt, joy instead of sadness, and that you give without conditions and love without expectations, and you will recognize that all that was told are qualities of heavenly bodies.

CHAPTER EIGHT

FAITH THE SHINING ARMOR, PEACE THE SHIELD AND SWORD

W hen we see ourselves as a separate drop of the ocean, we become lonely, disconnected, scared, egotistic, loveless, tyrannical, and ungrateful. When we see ourselves as an ocean in a drop, we become compassionate, connected to all, secure, loving, joyful, and peaceful.

Since a lot of our behavior stems from how we view ourselves in this universe, this is surly dedicated to my son who asked the question "where did god come from?" and walked away unsatisfied with his teacher's response that "you just have to have faith."

A good answer, but what does it mean? A thought after thought after thought . . . creates faith. So, in order to investigate faith, we must examine each thought that was used to generate that faith. However, where did that thought come from? Was it developed internally, without any external references, or was it a thought that you learned from other sources outside of yourself? If it came from an outside source, then is this your faith or their faith? Also, when you were given this thought, was it offered to you with the option for you to choose it, or was it forced as your only option to accept and follow?

Therefore, when we say "just have faith," it will mean something totally different to different people. Faith can save many and create miracles, or it can destroy many and abolish nations.

Hence, if faith cannot answer this question, then what would? It reminds me of this story: The monk went to his master and said, "Master, I have been to synagogues, churches, mosques, monasteries, temples, and solitudes, and cannot find God." His master smiled and said, "You will never find God because it is a discovery. Once you discover it within yourself, there will be no place that you will not find god."

So faith changes to discovery, and source is the source regardless of how you identify it. But where did it come from?

The best way to explain that is like this: Imagine I ask you a simple question that you know now but you did not know before, like what is ten times ten? It is one hundred. So simple and yet the answer presents itself so easily. Now, go back a few years to the time that you did not know what ten times ten was. Put yourself in that time and ask the same question with the knowledge that you had at that time. It would have been unimaginable, confusing, and chaotic to even think that two numbers multiplied by each other would have some kind of result, like one hundred that is perfect and is rationally accountable.

As time went by and your knowledge expanded, it led to the point of your discovery that ten can be multiplied by ten and produce another number that has a meaning and is perfectly accounted for, and it equals to one hundred.

Since our perception and daily training of living are oriented toward our physical experiences, it will be difficult to find a nonphysical source through physical experiences. Indeed, the option would be to have faith with prerequisite of discovery. Finding the source of the source requires looking from the eye of an I.

According to the NDE's (Near Death Experience) of many individuals who have been able to come back, we gain a 360-degree vision of all that is possible without a physical body. We see another dimension that we usually choose to ignore due to the loss of power through ego with distracted focus for the physical body. We recognize our true essence of freedom as we interpret that to be unconditional love and experience instant creation in absence of time.

And at this state of being, with this knowledge and discovery, we can easily answer how all started and see that all is well and there is an amazing order, harmony, and structure in the universe, as there is in ten times ten equals one hundred. Only then can we discover, appreciate, and develop faith for that source that beats our hearts. And no longer will we search for the source of the source, as a child feeling totally content in a mother's arms has no desire to search where the mother came from.

One may say there are not enough dimensions in language to describe "the source of the source."

Rumi said, "Although I may try to describe love, when I experience it, I am speechless."

When we have faith and believe, then the combustion of creation occurs as all becomes possible.

Belief is a thought after thought after thought that will give us that absolute vision of our reality. It is an absolute knowing about something that has not been contaminated with doubt, and it is the code that will allow us to access our energetic unlimited potentials of manifestation as desired, on demand.

We are born from an energetic environment that has no doubt, no limitation, no "good enough" issues, and that is worthy to receive all from an unlimited universe. One may say we are born without knowing anything about the belief because we have not learned about doubt yet. In absence of doubt, there is only belief.

Our brain, like a stock market expert, forecasts the future and prioritizes in order to only deal with most our body's demanding needs for our life experiences. Among the nearly 400 billion bits/second of information that it processes, only 2,000 bits/second are prioritized to be in our awareness, which mainly has to do with our immediate needs for environment and comfort. This forecasting of our needs is done automatically and energetically based on what our brain believes that we will need so the universe can provide it electromagnetically.

Like clouds moving from one location to another due to pressure changes and creating byproducts of rain, thunder and lightning, our thoughts, through the power of belief of what is needed, will cause different events to come to us as byproducts of our belief in order to create our reality.

In his book *The Biology of Belief*, Dr. Bruce Lipton explains about belief and its impact on our cells, genes, and health. Only 50 percent of our genes are inherited, and the other 50 percent are subject to change based on our belief. In multiple personality disorder patients, in one personality, the belief of having an allergy to a substance will be fatal, where in the same body but under a different personality, the belief has no impact.

Cold fusion, which provides the potential to create more energy from the same amount of energy, has shown that when the observer's belief is that it is possible, it will happen, and when the belief is that it cannot, then it will not happen.

Since belief is a thought after thought after thought, then it is important for us to investigate the quality of each thought individually to assure maintenance of the purity of our beliefs. If you wish to change your belief, examine and change every thought that created it in the first place. Be aware of the change that is needed and use affirmations to maintain it until it becomes the default thought. The best time to reaffirm your positive belief is just before you fall sleep or just before you wake up.

"Change how you look at things and things will change" is not just a poetic description of what we experience around us; it is the technology that teaches us that by changing our internal belief, our view of the world changes, and the manifestation of that change presents itself in all our surroundings and physical experiences.

"If I have the belief that I can do it, I shall surely acquire the capacity to do it even if I may not have it at the beginning." — MAHATMA GANDHI

Reason driven by fear keeps us in chains, but reason ignited by faith and belief allows us to recognize our true power as we fly, taking the quantum leap toward recognizing our true power.

Reason is the lighthouse that guides acceptance to shore. It is the gate that must be walked through in order to allow us to recognize love through conditional love, when we have forgotten our true essence of loving without conditions.

Through the training of life, we have gained knowledge in exchange for unconditional love. The left brain dictates that we must have reasons, while the energetic heart flows lovingly by experiencing the joy of going downstream. In a way, the heart has its own reasons that the brain will never understand.

We are born with a loving heart that loves unconditionally, without reasoning, same as a computer that has its own operating system ready to create whatever you wish it to create. It is the operator's choice to upload programs that are harmonious with this energy or in opposition to it.

When we develop our left brain in exchange for loss of our unconditional love, we develop a measuring system that we did not have before. Very soon we learn to evaluate and measure everything. Five is better than two, and ten is better than eight. You must be ten to value yourself, and if you are less than that, you are incomplete and must be inadequate. This will expand into assuming that you are too inadequate to love adequately. With this measuring system, the cup will never be full, and you will never be satisfied, not even when you reach ten. The trained left brain has been programmed to question, "What if there is eleven?" If there is, then you would still be inadequate.

However, with reason, you are allowed to guide yourself. With reason, you are allowed to walk out of the left-brain entrapment that you had guided yourself into in the first place. In the hierarchy of vibrational frequencies, it is neutrality, willingness, acceptance, reason, and conditional love before we enter unconditional love, joy, and peace, when we have been derailed from our true core.

Rumi said, "Your task is not to seek for love, but merely to seek and find all the barriers within yourself that you have built against it." Reason is the torch that allows you to recognize the barriers.

Reason is tricky and mischievous at times, since it is easily influenced by many things. Sometimes, we fool ourselves by fabricating a false reason for what appears to be the real reason. We hope to find an excuse to act a different way that is more conducive to what we mischievously prefer. This reason will eventually vanish and get superseded by the true reason, like a mirage since it is not real. We commonly refer to this recognition as wisdom.

"When Reason died, then Wisdom was born." — SRI AUROBINDO

When you enter a circular park and spend time walking on the trail and enjoying the flowers, the flowing river, the sound of the wind, the singing birds, and end near the same spot that you had started, you reach the point where you had begun. But that same spot of the beginning is no longer the beginning. All the reasons for the flowers, the river, the wind, and the birds have caused you to have wisdom. You no longer look at the trail the way you did before you had started, when standing at that same beginning.

"Had courage, wisdom, and reason always prevailed in people, there would not have been oppressions and oppressors." — AMEEN RIHANI

It is strange to comprehend that with less we can have more merely because we are accustomed to thinking that having more is better. Once we realize that we have not been created to own anything other than our thoughts, we find comfort in listening to the voice of silence that allows us to gain the knowledge of the universe.

Imagine eating sixty thousand times per day, the majority of it being the same food you had yesterday. Most likely your physical body will not tolerate such an overwhelming activity. Probably eating the same food alone every day will make it very unpleasant.

The average person has about sixty thousand thoughts per day, and the majority of their thoughts are the same defeating ones that they had yesterday. If our body requires a rest between meal times, then it makes sense to have some amount of rest time between our thought activities too.

Our major misconception is that we do not connect the signs of stress, such as depression, anxiety, fear, anger, insomnia, and other signs, with overactivity of our thoughts.

We work very much like a magnet. The electricity that passes through our body to keep us alive creates a current that develops a magnetic field around us. This magnetic field is the cause of attraction or repellent of our experiences with others, animals, nature, and the universe.

If we throw ten magnets on the floor, a few of them attract and the others repel each other based on how their polarities reacted as they got within a certain range. In a way, two cars that crash in an intersection while the other twenty cars passed by is not as random as it may appear.

Our thoughts have direct access to change this polarity by being parallel and harmonious with the universal flow of love and compassion or by opposing it. This magnetic field's interpretation presents itself internally as our state of health and externally as how we experience different events.

We can deliberately accomplish all the things that we desire and have experiences that are more conducive to our desires by being deliberate creators instead of living in a world of creation by default.

The first step in accomplishing the above is to manage our thoughts by slowing them down so we can monitor, detect, and analyze them. Meditation is the best process that can accomplish all of that, in addition to maximizing our universal default energy flow due to elimination of resistive thoughts. Also, meditation can be qualified as a compass that allows us to evaluate our direction before we become obsessed with how fast we can proceed. What good is it to drive very fast but in the wrong direction?

There are many different methods of meditation; however, we must recognize that more procedures about how to relax may become stressful and counterproductive.

- *Preparation*: Find a comfortable environment and position without distraction and with proper rhythmic breathing.
- *Meditation for relaxation*: Start from the toes and progress up the body in small sections. With each breath, bring in new vital energy. With each exhale, discharge any stress from that part of the body to the universe.

- *Meditation for purification*: Hold a lit candle about two feet away from your face at eye level. Open your eyes a little more than comfortable and gaze at the gap at the bottom of the flame. Do not blink; maintain this position. Allow the impurities of your eyes to drop down as tears (do not rub them). As soon as you blink, stop and wash off the tears. Let any thoughts that come up during this process pass through without holding on to them, as they are discharging from your head to the universe or through your tears.

- *Meditation for appreciation*: Appreciation is our default state where we cease to be superior or inferior and simply are present. Quietly, simply, and humbly thank the universal energy that beats your heart for all the events of your hour, day, month, year, or any special occasions. Recognize that the universe's default is always well, regardless of how you may interpret it at that time, and offer thanks for each experience. Find something positive about each event as you go through them.

- *Meditation for manifestation*: Close your eyes and draw a large imaginary circle a few feet in front of you. Put a single thought of what you desire in the center of the circle. Move any other distracting thoughts outside the circle as they come up by keeping your focus on the single thought inside the circle. Also, this can be enhanced by the flow of breathing through second chakra (at below belly button) up to sixth chakra (at about the bridge of nose / 3rd eye) and projecting your exhale to the center of the circle.

(Note: The above can also be modified by breathing up via the 2nd chakra and allowing it to vibrate inside the center of your head behind 6th chakra following the sound of exhale with Ahhh and ending with Ommm.)

Now that we understand all the prerequisites of finding the direction to our path, how can we ensure that we maintain this course and reach our desired goals? Have you ever wondered why you fall short of reaching your goals?

It seems that all the desire, energy, excitement, and willingness is there to make it happen at the beginning, but by the time we get to the terminus, we realize that we are far from the goal we had originally planned for.

It's like looking down a road, bright as a sunny day with our goal at the end of it, calling us to get there to embrace it. Somehow as we start travelling down this path, many things happen that derail us from the destination.

At times the light goes out and we find ourselves lost in this darkness, not knowing how to find our goal. Amazingly, sometimes a light appears from nowhere and gives us the visibility we need to see our goal again, so we can head in its direction.

I call these moments the candles that light our way when we are lost and derailed. These quotations from past masters redirect us by lighting our path like a candle, and all the darkness in the world cannot stop its radiance.

Candle 1: "Early in the morning as he (Jesus) was on his way back from the city, he saw a fig tree by the road. He went up toward it but found nothing on it except leaves. Then he said to it, "May you never bear fruit again." Immediately, the tree withered. When the disciples saw this, they were amazed. "How did the fig tree whither so quickly?" they asked. Jesus replied, "I tell you the truth. If you have faith and do not doubt, not only can you do what was done to the fig tree, but you can also tell this mountain to go throw itself into the sea and it will be done, if you believe you will receive whatever you ask for in prayers."

Candle 2: During the day, different occasions may arise that may require reminding yourself of Thoreau's quote regarding success. This can bring clarity to your goals and redirect your focus toward what is desired: "If one advances confidently in the direction of his dreams, and endeavors to live the life which he has imagined, he will meet with a success unexpected in common hours."

Candle 3: Sometimes an occasion arises that requires acting independent of the opinions of others. The change comes when we act beyond the environment and what is considered comfortable and the norm. Thinking outside the box requires patience and an understanding of being inside the box first. This Emerson quote will guide you to act independent of others' opinions, to be aligned with what is universally and energetically considered right: "Do not go where the path may lead, go instead where there is no path and leave a trail."

Candle 4: Finally, you will need to recognize that you are love, you are loving, and you are beyond that, and any type of fear will lessen that absolute truth about who you truly are, since you were born to be fearless. When all the thoughts, news, propaganda, and unspoken fear of the surrounding environment becomes apparent, it is time to remind yourself of the old man who told his children the following at his deathbed (as was noted earlier): "I have had many troubles in my life, but most of them never happened."

There is a simple secret to happiness, unconditional love, and compassion that is so obvious, yet many of us never discover it. We are born with it but somehow we redirect from its path.

It reminds me of the thief who followed a diamond merchant on a train and stayed near him all day and night, trying to steal his diamond to no success. At the end of the trip, he said, "Diamond merchant, I am a thief and I have been trying to steal your diamond all this time and knew that you had one, but I could not find it. Where did you hide it?" The diamond merchant smiled, reached inside the thief's pocket, and said, "I hid it inside your own pocket because I knew you would never look there." The secret of our joy, happiness, love, and compassion is hidden inside where we rarely look for it. Remember that "you have no issues, you only think you do" (from the book and program called ACIM "*A Course in Miracles*").

When we see ourselves as a drop of the ocean, we feel insignificant when looking at our inadequacy and existence and place in this universe. We want to become the ocean and search, evaluate, and compare ourselves with other drops, hoping that one day we become the ocean. This becomes a constant struggle to evaluate and compare ourselves with others. We go to extremes to estimate and equate ourselves with constantly being unsatisfied.

Since we can never be the ocean and the concept has fundamental fallacy, we will never be satisfied, regardless of how much we try to make ourselves a bigger drop of this ocean, whether by gaining more money, fame, power, prestige, beauty, and more, or by comparing ourselves to other drops.

Miraculously, somehow, we become tired of this struggle and finally realize that we are not a drop of the ocean but instead "we are the entire ocean in a drop," as Rumi noted, with all its power and perfection. It is same as our physical gene, which carries many of our parents' physical features, yet it is so small and hidden at conception.

Once we discover this, we cease all searches and inquires, since we no longer desire to search for our inadequacies to find our place in this universe, as we are finally completely at peace. With this knowledge, every day becomes a new day of enjoyment of this beautiful experience we call life.

When you see yourself as the entire ocean in a drop, you realize that there is nothing missing, and all is well.

You will choose joy at every opportunity that life provides. You recognize that you have power at the space that exists between each thought and your action that allows you to elect wisely. You realize that happiness is a byproduct of your choice, and you return to your essence of loving without conditions.

CHAPTER NINE

BLISS, I CAN HEAR CLEARLY NOW!

W e come from a spiritual world and start from a physical dot that begins us. It is said that our evolvement has four stages. First, we see what we can do with our bodies, how strong or beautiful they can become. Then we try to gather as many materialistic things as possible. Third is when we ask how we may be of service to others, and the last stage is when we realize that we are spiritual beings having physical experiences, rather than the other way around, as we go back to the world we came from.

It appears that all creation is cyclical. The Earth, the planets, the flow of universe, the four seasons—they end where they had begun. All the ends appear to start at the same beginning, but somehow that beginning is no longer the same. The observer has gained some profound knowledge that was not available before.

So how does this circle begin and end? How do we find ourselves back at where we had begun, but with a different perception from that eye of an I? It appears to be the same beginning, yet totally different and full of things that we had no comprehension of nor the capacity to understand before.

We come from an energetic world knowing that all our desires will become reality. We have the understanding that our energetic power allows us to put all our desires into a vibrational escrow, awaiting conception in our experiences. This conception may only happen when we are prepared to receive and experience them, when we feel ready to allow them to come through.

Somehow along the way, we become doubtful of this reality and it seems that our desires get further and further away from us until we hear a silent voice deep within. This voice sounds so familiar that it seems like we have known each other forever, and it assures us that all is well, that all will be well, and that all will happen just the way we want it. "Just wait and see, be patient and try again. You can do it, it will happen soon, you'll see!"

Suddenly we recognize that we have forgotten who we truly are. We are spiritual beings having physical experiences, not the other way around, and we are not limited by boundaries. We are reminded to unfold our full capabilities and reach for all that we desire without limitations. We suddenly break the barriers that we have built by our own thoughts in order to prove to ourselves that we are incapable. This voice within us causes us to spring up to reach for the sky, and we soar to fly again.

"Hope, my good old friend, my companion, my teacher, the voice inside echoed by the cheering of unknown divine faces within my soul, and Hope, my cane that I have leaned on through all my struggles, let me embrace you and never let go. It is good to see you again."-By author.

Dr. Newton, in his book *Journey of Souls*, documents his research with people who had been hypnotized and had reported their experiences after their previous deaths. The experiences conclude that we do not and cannot bring all our energetic part back with us to have physical experiences, and we leave a part of our energetic being in the energetic field.

This means that every physical experience will only have a percentage of our total being in physical form, while the other percentage stays in the energetic field but is directly connected to our physical parts. This energetic part is what we return to after our physical experiences are over. In a way, if we assume that we only bring 75 percent of our energetic being to have physical experiences, the other 25 percent remains in that field but is always connected to us, and guides us at all times to remind us of who we truly are. When we return to this state of being, we recognize that our completed 100 percent energy is not separated from others and that we all belong together like a web in the universe. Our 25 percent side is always aware of the unity of all and the grace of the source that beats all hearts without partiality. However, our physical part is reconditioned by fears and separates itself from others through ego and loss of true vision of the universe and the absolute truth.

Regardless of our belief regarding such studies, the correlations are high that we all sense a teacher guiding us, a silent voice giving us hope, an angel showing us things when we need it, a silent whisper telling us that all will be fine and that regardless of how terrified we are, there is always hope, assuring us that it will all be OK and all will be taken care of. It is the caretaker who we never see. Maybe it is time for us to end where we had begun: Hope, my old friend, it is good to see you again!

It appears that we all have the same essence and go through the same conceptual process of physical and emotional growth. We are the same ocean in a drop heading back to the ocean with an energetic entanglement that, once recognized, will end all questions.

In the 1930s, scientific society along with Einstein were puzzled and surprised by the results of an experiment known as "Entanglement."

They separated two atoms by several thousand miles. Then they excited one atom and monitored the results of the other atom. It was shocking to find out that the other atom instantly showed the exact same excitement, as if they were never separated. This showed that once two atoms are entangled energetically, they sync together and behave the same way, as if they were one but in two separate physical locations, regardless of their distance.

The most basic example of this marvel is how we are physically born. There is an entanglement between every mother and child that is undeniable. Science may not be able to explain many aspects of this, but the evidence of it exists in each of our hearts. We have all been children and have posed the same questions to our mothers many times, regardless of how old we were—"How did you know that?" or "How could you have possibly ever known that?" and more.

If this entanglement exists between each mother and child and is energetic, then the first law of thermodynamics tells us that energy will never die and it only changes phase as it transfers to something different independent from time. Since this bond surpasses time energetically, it cannot be limited to a physical lifetime, as it passes through all lifetimes. Subsequently, all mothers will be energetically entangled along with all their children. Eventually this will lead to that source mother that started it all and proves that there is an entanglement among all of us.

Many people with NDEs (Near Death Experience) have defined this vision of timeless entanglement among all beings as a tapestry. Each thread of this tapestry is each of our lives, each with a specific location, color, story, and shape unique to itself impacting the tapestry's pattern. Each thread specifically needs to be just the way it is, otherwise it will impact the tapestry as a whole. As each thread changes, the other threads will change accordingly. Even though each thread may not understand why it has to have a certain color or shape or location within the larger image of the tapestry as a whole. However, the tapestry's overall image is always beautiful, as the artist who planned it was looking at all of it to make sure that it is well coordinated.

Whether we look through a microscope to find our source within the tiniest matter or look through a telescope to the end of the universe to justify our being, we find the origin of this entanglement back to that energy that beats all our hearts.

"It is the strangest thing, it doesn't matter where you are in the world, or how much time we have spent apart, I always feel this connection, like our souls are entangled—like we are two rivers winding alongside one another, sometimes in separate directions, but always toward the ocean." — BEAU TAPLIN

In order to see creation from the same angle that the creator does, we must give up the illusion that we are our bodies. To travel down this path, one may begin by asking the question, "Do you need your body?"

This may sound like a silly question at first, but if you think about it, you will conclude that all your decisions have been made based on how you internally answer this very profound yet basic question. Once you have an opinion about your relationship to your body, then from that point on, all your decisions will be pivoted accordingly.

Also, when you evaluate some of the events of your life, you will notice that many of your actions and reactions have been mainly based on protecting this body or maintaining the image you have of it.

So, the fundamental question would be, what is your relationship with your body? Do you think that you are your body? Or do you think that you are separated from your body and mainly reside in it for the short time of your physical life experiences?

Some of the studies that measured people just before and after their death reported that a dead person loses an average of a few ounces right after their death. While this has been controversial as far as being interpreted to be the weight of our soul, the fact of its existence cannot be denied.

Many sects of yogis and monks require that their novices train in meditation practices that simulate their physical death so they can remove that fear and avoid becoming hostage to it through their growth in search for enlightenment.

As was noted earlier; "To embrace is to love, and to let go is to love more. Knowing that the desire to hold is to possess, and to possess is to rule, and to rule is to be separated, and separation is to be apart from ourselves, to part from ourselves is to be independent from the divine force that created us, and to be alone in an endless universe can only be described as hell as we know it."

So, to embrace the body that we temporarily reside in is still to love, but to be capable of not being attached to it is to love even more. This presents a profound understanding of who we are and our unlimited potentials, which only become available when recognized by each of us individually welcoming all other possibilities without allowing our relationship with our bodies to stop us. Thus, if you were this body, the next logical question would be, "Will you get upset when you die?"

Imagine it is winter and someone you are very fond of but do not know well has invited you to a summer party at their house in a few months. You try to find out as much as possible about this person's taste and what he is like during the time that you have, so you can buy just the right gift to impress him. The day of the party comes and you walk in to find out that the gift in your hand is in total clash with who you thought he was and is not something that he would ever use or have any attraction to. Do you get upset that you went through all that trouble and hardship when you could have bought a different gift that would have been more compatible, if you had only known better?

Similarly, you live about one hundred years and gather all this information about what your life is supposed to be about and where you might go after you die based on information that all living people have provided you with. Will you get upset when you die to find out that those priorities were not important and not anything like what was propagandized, almost as though you had lived a backward life?

As was previously mentioned, Dr. Michael Newton's *Journey of Souls* is one of my favorite books, along with many other similar ones, that has documented the experiences of many people before they were born and after they had previously died through hypnosis.

According to Newton and through his research, many of us will get upset when we die and look at the life that we had lived, distracted by things that had no importance. However, the good news is that without a physical body, it is hard to be upset, so the experience will be more like a learning process than any punishment that we can relate to, and more similar to the disappointment of not bringing the right gift for the party mentioned above.

He further documents that these disappointments come from our overview of our time on Earth when we realize that we had preoccupied ourselves with our body, its shape, its color; separations among nations; war, fear, money, prestige, hatred, and more, instead of enjoying breath, life, the beauty of Earth, nature, companionship, love, friendship, unification of humanity, and celebration of our unity in the same spirit as a whole as it is in our energetic nonphysical form.

Who says we need a body to live? It is mainly a misconception that defines this experience as we continue living with other experiences later.

The Indian spiritual master, Sai Baba said, "Life is a song—sing it. Life is a game—play it. Life is a challenge—meet it. Life is a dream—realize it. Life is a sacrifice—offer it. Life is love—enjoy it."

Too many questions and not enough answers. So, how can we always have the right answer to these questions and all others that come up along this path of self-inquiry to find the voice within?

"To the man who only has a hammer, everything he encounters begins to look like a nail!". — ABRAHAM MASLOW

How are we absolutely sure that we have the right answer, and yet later regret that it was not the right one? We make decisions at every moment based on what we know, including our biases and unconscious preferences.

The four steps below will ensure that all our answers will be right with complete certainty, regardless of conditions and time:

1. Einstein said, "All I want is to be able to think like God does." In order to think like God does, we need to approach our question from wholeness and without feelings of fear, need, lack, and inadequacy.

2. Our answer will need to be imbedded in the fullness that includes all love and no fear.

3. In order to understand God's wholeness, we cannot simulate that completeness with half a brain, whether it is the left analytical brain or the creative right brain. We have to approach our answer with our entire brain. Compassion is the glue that connects the left brain and right brain together as a whole. So, our answer will need to be reached by opening the door to compassion.

4. Saint Francis said, "All the darkness in the world cannot extinguish the light of a single candle." The right answer may not be the popular one, but it will be the absolute right one, consistent with universal flow and intentions when it was made based on the above. So, we will need to act independent from the opinions of others, regardless of their popularity, in order to have the absolute true answer.

Based on these simple steps, it seems so simple to find the absolute unconditional right answer for every question when it is made with trinity of love, compassion, and freedom.

Finally, now that we have assurance in our ability to find the right answers every time, we are prepared to look for the key to happiness.

A law is defined as something that is absolute and always works, regardless of variables and conditions. The law of universe indicates that the energy that beats our hearts, beats all hearts without discrimination or any partiality with fluency.

Swimming upstream is considered friction, compared to going with the flow and enjoying the ride downstream. This means that we interpret this fluent, joyful, downstream feeling as happiness.

However, our attitude toward interpreting what we may consider as being upstream or downstream will impact this happiness.

Our happiness is mainly experienced during the times that we act as "deliberate creators," not the times when we find ourselves imprisoned by the conditions imposed by the belief of being stuck in the world of "creation by default" to be out of control.

In a way, we may say that the key to happiness is when we act as "deliberate creators," since this downstream flow of energy seems to be the universal law of harmonic balance between our desires and our received experiences.

How do you monitor yourself to maintain this happiness, as your desires and what you receive in response to them changes at different times?

You consciously or unconsciously oscillate between the two polarities of love and fear that may be summed up to be within the following four conditions that were described earlier in chapter 4:

1. *You are happy and you want to be happy.*

2. *You are happy and for some reason you want to be miserable.*

3. *You are miserable and you want to be miserable.*

4. *You are miserable and you want to be happy.*

It appears that happiness is a statue that comes alive and develops its own personality only when we recognize the gift of thankfulness.

Man's Search for Meaning by Viktor Frankl provides priceless information learned through painful, unconscionable experiences. Dr. Frankl was a psychiatrist who was sent to concentration camps during the Holocaust. His food consisted of hot water with a floating fish head for flavor, and he experienced many other forms of abuse.

He realized that in a place where only a few could survive, the key to survival and withstanding the abuse was not food nor strength. It was the gift of finding meaning in our daily lives, finding beauty in everything (even in the dead fish head) and having hope to be thankful, without hating the capturers.

Dr. Frankl revolutionized the previous theories of human behavior established by Nietzsche and Freud as being the "the will to power" and "the will to pleasure." Nietzsche's concept had previously defined the human being's purpose and motivation in life to be success, accomplishments, goals, power, and reaching the highest position in life. Freud believed that seeking pleasure and avoiding pain drove us to have hope to be alive and have the will to live.

Frankl realized that the other two concepts may have been important, but at their roots they were empty and false, since they will never truly satisfy our real nature; our real fulfillment comes from love, and any lack of love is fear, which will cause us to pursue the other two concepts in search of a mirage of happiness.

Frankl, the father of logotherapy, introduced the new principal that our main motivation to live is not power nor pleasure, but to find meaning in life. This included "meaning" under all circumstances, even the most miserable ones. Basically, he discovered that a lot of pleasure, power, and success, and a sense of accomplishment are created when we find meaning in our life, but approaching it from the other direction alone will give us false meanings that lead to unhappiness and will never be satisfying.

Leo Tolstoy, in his beautiful novella *The Death of Ivan Ilyich*, tells the story of a successful judge in Moscow who had everything but hated many, including his own family members. As he became sick, his view of life changed, and with his last breath he asked his wife, "What if everything that I have always believed was wrong?" It is unimaginable to live one hundred years with uncertainty, that all we have believed in was wrong.

"We have freedom to find meaning in what we do and what we experience, or at least in the stand we take when faced with a situation of unchangeable suffering." — TENET OF LOGOTHERAPY

They say one of the most unique things about Mother Teresa was that when she walked in villages full of filth, sorrow, disease, and pain, instead of focusing on all of the unpleasant things that were apparent to others, she was always able to find a little flower or something else, and appreciated its beauty and was thankful.

"There are only two ways to live your life. One is as though nothing is a miracle. The other is as though everything is a miracle." — ALBERT EINSTEIN

Based on the above, the following becomes meaningful: giving thanks for all we have through this beautiful experience that we call life, and asking forgiveness for the times that we detached ourselves by our aggressions toward any living being when we felt lost, unwanted, hurt, lonely, and separated from the unity that we share as being the absolute truth.

When do we find this source that began them all and is the fountain and the ocean that we feed from and will return to?

As the master told his student previously who was looking to find god; "You will never find God because it is a discovery. Once you discover it within yourself, there will be no place that you will not find god."

We discover the force that beats our hearts and is much closer to us than any external being, even our parents who gave us our lives:

- When we walk in a garden, stop by every flower and appreciate the differences of each flower, each uniqueness, then continue to a crowded place and have the same appreciation and respect for each person that we come in contact with, and view their differences as the essence of their beauty.

- When we realize that we cannot own anything other than our thoughts. We realize that it is great to have all the toys that we desire, but it is even greater when we share them, since we are leasing them for a short while and will return them soon.

- When we see someone in distress and feel their pain as ours, and without looking to place blame or to discover why they deserve to receive that experience, we reach out to help and then tell them to not give it back, but to pass it forward.

- When we realize the perfection of the universe and that all is well, and nothing is missing. We realize that this life is only one chapter of our story, and like any other book, we can not understand it by analyzing only one chapter.

- When we realize that separation between people, neighbors, nations, and countries is far from the universal intention of the grace that flows without hesitation and partiality. We recognize the fallacy of our justifications and understand that no war nor separation can be possibly done in the name of God, that everything but peace stems from our personal need to satisfy ego, and that angry people cannot create a peaceful world.

- When we are inspired to create and to inspire others everywhere we go. We go to sleep with appreciation for the beautiful experience of the day we had, and anxiously wake to enjoy the best day of our lives, knowing that every moment of "now" is a "present."

- When we have faith as the song birds do when they sing before seeing the sunrise, knowing that the sun always shines, and we are always connected and never disconnected.

The little boy who was doing many miracles was called to the village elders. They said he surely knew where God is. The elders said, "We will give you an apple if you show us where he is." The boy responded, "I will give you two apples if you show me where he is not."

CHAPTER TEN

THE VOICES WITHIN

As I Lay Me Down to Sleep

There is a magical moment where each of us has the power to energetically make a change to our attitude, personality, health, happiness, and any aspect of what is desired. This moment is just before we fall sleep and just before we wake up.

Once we recognize the power of this moment, we can create all that is desired at will under our direct control, since we are able to consciously direct our subconscious.

Ego is the part of our energetic field created to protect the body. It kicks you in the morning and demands that you are this body, so get up and feed me. Also, it is the part of us that we must give up at night in order to fall asleep.

We operate at our nearly full capacity as spiritual beings having physical experiences when our ego is at minimum. We move near the speed of light where diseases do not exist, as this state of pure energy transforms based on the power of "be and it is" without time delay.

Therefore, the quality of our thoughts as we fall asleep and as we wake up have great importance. We can all attest to our pleasant or unpleasant experiences that we have had through dreams, and otherwise through feelings, when we have had good or bad thoughts just before falling asleep and just before waking up.

Our brain activity drops down from beta to alpha to theta to delta as we fall asleep, and reverses as we start waking up.

We have a small window of opportunity to interject a thought in the low beta-alpha level activity of the brain with the possibility that will be carried down to theta automatically. This will start becoming more energetic, and magical things will begin to happen as we reach theta and delta at our purest energetic state.

The aforementioned means that we can follow a certain routine that will be more conducive to directing our subconscious willingly and efficiently. These routines are summarized in the following steps:

- Avoid any kind of screen interactions in bed.

- Avoid focusing on any negative thought, fear, or worry before falling asleep and when getting up.

- Meditate before falling asleep to reduce the beta-level activity of the brain.

- Do any form of prayer, meditation, mantra, etc., acceptable to you that promotes appreciation for the day's events independent from how good or bad they were.

- Form a short, positive, single thought for what is desired and repeat it as you fall asleep and continue it immediately upon waking up. Assume the feeling of what this desire is the best you can, as if you already have it when you fall asleep.

The Pruning Shears of Revision: Every day, before you go to sleep, think through the events of the day. If any events or moments did not go the way you wanted, replay them in your mind in a way that thrills you. As you recreate those events in your mind exactly as you want, you are cleaning up your frequency from the day and you are emitting a new signal and frequency for tomorrow. You have intentionally created new pictures for your future. It is never too late to change the pictures. — NEVILLE GODDARD

Awakened from Being "Awake"

When we have a dream, our absolute reality is the belief that it is real. When we wake, we then realize it was just a dream. Our dreams are so real that they change our bodily functions; they change our emotions; they make us feel sad, happy, angry, loving, hurt, frightened, and more. They can even give us intimacy with a partner who has no physical existence upon awakening.

What if the same exists when you are awake? The limitations that you believe are real only exist in this unawaken state of not recognizing your true essence of power. It only exists because you do not realize who you truly are. Once you wake up from this state of being awake, you realize that those limitations never existed. The source that beats your heart has no limitations, has no boundary, has no inadequacy, and will reach all that's desired without any doubts. It has no state of dis-ease, since disease does not exist in energy.

When we see glimpses of this true awakening beyond our belief, we call them miracles as being extraordinary. However, in reality those are the moments when we wake up from this state of being awake to see our true power that is a part of our ordinary state of being.

There are many organizations that investigate the authenticity of the events that we call miracles. There are thousands of these miracles that cannot be explained by science and are shielded by our normal state of deception from recognizing our true power. Among those, there are a few that may be noted here to exemplify our state of awakening, once we recognize our true capabilities:

- What causes a woman who had deformed knees, and who had been in a wheelchair for years, to reach for her true power? She asks to have perfect health from that source without doubt and without any barrier. This time it is different as she crosses the barrier that she had not crossed before. Within seconds, she feels an unknown pain and tingling in her feet. Within a few minutes, her deformed knee is in perfect alignment and she is able to walk and climb up the stairs to inform her family that she had walked upstairs by herself in perfect health. The doctors and science are still puzzled by the before and after X-rays that show her knees had magically healed.

- What about the woman who is technically certified as blind without her thick glasses? Her daughter, who has been missing for three months, calls frantically after taking an overdose. She fails to give her mother the address before she passes out. The mother breaks her glasses as she tries to reach for the phone. She follows her instincts and drives to where she is guided, driving without her glasses to an unknown location based on her intuition, and makes it to the exact room where her daughter is, just in time to save her life.

- What about the criminal who had removed the battery of a woman's car to trap her inside a secluded parking garage? Her car does not start. When she cries with her absolute belief of being delivered to safety, the universe organizes all the events, even beyond the laws of physics, to start her car without a battery to take her to safety. To the attacker's amazement, the car starts and she drives home. Her husband investigates the problem with the car and is baffled by the possibility of the car driving home without the battery.

Rumi said, "What strange beings we are, sitting at the bottom of dark, afraid of our own immortality."

"Maybe life is a childish game of hide and seek that once we are tired of hiding, the desire to be found springs up from the roots of our beings to become awaken from being awake."
— FROM THE AUTHOR

Can You Love a Monster?

Every piece of equipment comes with an operating manual. No equipment is ever sold with the expectation that the operator will create the operating manual as they learn to operate that piece of equipment. If there was ever a piece of equipment marketed that way, it would be considered poor planning to promote and expand such equipment. The human creation, body, and psyche, along with the rest of creation in the universe, is considered to be the most sophisticated and complex machinery and technology that we have ever known. Assuming that the creator who has capabilities to provide such perfection and technology has not thought of arranging for an operating manual with it seems improbable.

We must assume that the original architect of this creation has included some form of operating manual independent from the one that has been influenced by the operators, independent from what was thought and assumed to be the right one by others, and independent from different groups' assumptions and interpretations. An operating manual that is considered the law of universe and applicable to all conditions. This means that this manual must have been included with each package at birth, independent from all the above.

Indeed, we are all born with such an operating manual embedded in us at birth through our energetic creation. Somehow, we are derailed from it as we interact with others. We lose contact with our operating manual and follow some directions that were developed and learned by operators different than what was intended to be the absolute default.

There is a program called *A Course in Miracles*. It is a magical program and series of books and information that should be taught to all children before teaching them A, B, C and 1, 2, 3. It is the closest operating manual that can be presumed to be prepared from the architect who planned it all. Regardless of having or not having any religion or belief, the course touches you and evokes that part of you to question any behavior that is fear-driven, leading to lack of loving and uncompassionate behavior.

One of my favorite parts of the course is the following, where it offers a different point of view from an angle that may not be apparent to many. In one of the large group sessions, one of the counselors teaches about the importance of how we are to love everyone as our core essence. An older lady in the audience questions this and responds, "Are you saying that we have to even love a monster? I will never love Adolf Hitler." The numbered tattoo on her arm indicates that she had directly experienced the horror of the Holocaust.

The instructor pauses before responding to the old lady. "Imagine a little boy who has been abused by his alcoholic father on daily basis. Imagine a little boy who has to take care of his mentally ill mother on daily basis. Imagine a little boy who has been ridiculed daily by all his neighbors because of these things. Can you love this little boy?"

The old lady is silent for a while, then she responds with quiet shaken voice, "Yes."

The instructor continues. "Do you believe that if that little boy was ever loved a little, he would have ever grown up to be a monster?"

The operating manual imbedded in all of us as individuals, parents, tyrants, victims, and monsters came with a simple instruction to "love a little." In our confusion, we have lost our connection with the absolute truth that love is generated from self to self, stemming from the energy that beats our hearts independent from what we may all call it. It can only overflow when the cup overflows.

Deception of Addiction and Solution

Consuming alcohol or other substances is one of the largest and oldest practices around the world. Many people are happy and drink alcohol or use other substances same as soda, cakes, and other consumable items because they simply enjoy it and maintain their happiness with or without it. Some occasionally drink it when they feel stressed and look for the relief that it provides, like a massage or classical music, or a warm cup of tea or other relaxing options that are available.

However, some are considered emotional drinkers and drink in search of a solution that they hope to find in the bottle. They use alcohol to feel better and, in their misery, they view the numbness that it provides as a state of temporary relief confused by the solution to be happier in comparison to their current state of discomfort. They get more and more attached to this deception as the source of relief. It is like walking down the street and finding a hole, thinking that if you dig a hole where you are standing, you can use the dirt to fill the hole in front of you, not realizing the new hole that you are creating, and sinking into it.

Independent from how they got there, there is an energetic absolute answer that describes all causes. Equally, there is an energetic absolute answer that will pull them out from the belief that this deception is their only option.

Regardless of our religious beliefs and what we may call the source of the energy that wirelessly, electromagnetically makes our heart beat, we each do have a heartbeat that creates our unique experiences as our reality. When this electrical energy flows through our body with very little stress, we feel exalted and light, as if we have no body; we hear the music when no one is playing, and we are joyful, happy, and at ease. When we experience any physical or emotional stress, we become denser, slower, heavier, sluggish, unwell, unhappy, uncomfortable, and dis-eased.

David Hawkins, in his book *Power vs. Force*, masterfully defines the levels of emotional stress, from most to least stressful, as shame, guilt, apathy, grief, fear, desire, anger, pride, courage, neutrality, willingness, acceptance, reason, love, unconditional love, joy, and peace. In a way, when you experience shame, the only way to go up the ladder to get to joy and peace is through the door of experiencing guilt, apathy, and other emotions as you process yourself out of that shameful emotion. It can be done very fast without any residue left behind, or it can be done very slow with many unresolved issues left behind that force you to come back and be stuck in each of those levels over and over again. The good news is that it is totally up to you and what you choose.

Most alcoholics get stuck in the emotions of shame and guilt. They reach to apathy (hopelessness) for relief and then somehow get exposed to alcohol. Because alcohol temporarily makes them go up the ladder to experience grief, fear, desire, and anger during their short time of intoxication, they find this deception to be their solution and relief. Soon, they have to reach for it more and more as they develop a tolerance to its absorption, same as digging themselves in a deeper and deeper hole in the example mentioned above.

Change comes when we act beyond our environment and what we are accustom to. This means realizing that moving up the emotional ladder is an available choice at any moment and does not need any substance to go through those steps. Sometimes, this is best when guided by a professional or knowledgeable friend who understands the progression of those steps, and sometimes individuals can find the way on their own as they can no longer tolerate the discomfort.

Since the highest stress levels are shame and guilt, and the key to releasing both of them is through forgiveness of ourselves and others, the forgiveness meditations posted in previous chapters or other similar techniques such as; EMDR (Eye Movement Desensitization and Reprocessing), EFT (Emotional Freedom Therapy), Grief Therapy, and Time Line Therapy will be very productive. Yoga, breathing, physical activities, and practices to stop the vicious cycle of defeating thoughts will be great companions as they eventually recognize the power within as the need for external substances vanishes. Understanding the ladder noted above is a must in order to remove any confusion and fear along the way.

Sometimes, the best way to allow irritation to pass is to experience it by simply, patiently, and lovingly allowing yourself to be irritated without justifying it, without making excuses, and with love and compassion. Recognize that love can only be generated from self to self and can only be extended to others when it has overflown from the individual. Love heals all wounds and flows when you align with the energy that beats your heart without any resistance. It is your essence, it is time to come back home and be comforted that you are whole and no external substance can ever make you whole. The wholeness that you have been missing is the pearl inside waiting to be found. It was placed their at your birth and all you need is to look inside and quietly whispering its code "Love" to open its shell'.

Determination to Succeed!

Gandhi said, "First they ignore you, then they laugh at you, then they fight you, then you win."

We are all enthused by the goals we set and the results we get as we succeed to grow and to continue our expansion. However, many of us fall short of succeeding to reach the desired target.

Many athletes attend the Olympics but only one receives the gold medal. The athletes have trained their muscles to the point of exhaustion and saturation, many times over the years, as far as physically possible. The muscle training will eventually reach its maximum capacity and equalize among all competitors. However, there is a level that is beyond the physical body's limitation that determines the success of reaching the destination beyond all obstacles.

The greatest mathematician of all time, Einstein, was not a baseball player. The most famous baseball player of all time, Babe Ruth, was not a mathematician. Each had chosen to focus with complete enthusiastic determination on excelling in their desired tasks. They both had been ignored, laughed at, fought against by those opposing them, and they struggled to finally win.

> "The difference between the impossible and the possible lies
> in a man's determination." — TOMMY LASORDA

So, what is this magic potion of determination that makes it all possible? How can we have it and how do we know if we do not have it?

The answer is simple. It is rooted in all of us as our essence. As energetic beings, all our creations are based on our expectation to have all that is desired to be materialized at the speed of light. At this timeless state, determination is instant and does not require to be maintained since there is an unmeasurable fraction of time that is being elapsed. In a way, in this state all our creation is with complete determination.

When this energetic part of us that has nothing but determination mixes with our physical side that has the limitations of mass and time delays, the outcome becomes a mixture of both. When our driving force is more physical, then the determination fails, and when the driving force is more energetic, the energetic part of us, determination, will push through to succeed.

Miyamoto Musashi was one of the greatest samurais of Japan's 16th century. When he was faced with his greatest battle to the death, he said he knew that both had drawn their swords thousands of times and there was nothing that he could do more to succeed physically. His only strategy was to win his opponent in his mind. The samurai duel is a very formal ceremony that begins to show mastery by whomever is dressed better and is more punctual to attend the ceremony. Musashi showed up late, wearing casual clothes and with a wooden sword to dishonor his challenger. By the time the duel had started, he had already won the battle in his opponent's mind. With determination we transition from discipline to mastery with 1,000 days of lessons for discipline, 10,000 days of lessons for mastery.

Determination is when we maintain the desired path under all conditions to overflow the cup with what is desired and to keep our eyes on the target without being distracted under all conditions. "When everyone else says you can't, determination says, yes you can."-Unknown.

> "Using no way as a way, having no limitation
> as limitation." — BRUCE LEE

Freedom from Emotional Hostage

Have you ever been self-conscious about something when interacting with others? It appears that one thing becomes your dominate thought, holding you hostage and changing your interactions from a balanced, equal relationship to something imbalanced and less for you.

Some common examples include being concerned about your weight or height, thinking that you are too smart or not smart enough, worrying about having too much money or not having enough, being preoccupied with your skin color, meeting a certain status or falling short of it, being attractive or not attractive enough, and more.

The labels we have learned to measure ourselves with have become the source of how we value ourselves. Soren Kierkegaard said, "Once you label me, you negate me." Because of these labels, we more often become apologetic for no reason. It seems like being held hostage by the emotion that follows each label as we feel the lack and mourn the wholeness that is our joyful essence.

A hostage is one who is held against their will by not having the freedom to say and do the things that they desire. This may be among different people, or it can happen among the four energetic bodies of each individual internally, as each impacts the other within the same body.

Our four energetic bodies are physical, emotional, psychological, and spiritual. The interaction of these four bodies make us whole in being in peace and joyful or, in contrast with each other, in dis-ease. Many of the new computerized energy programs, such as Biowell, are able to measure the energetic flow of each finger and forecast their data very accurately to identify the culprit elements among these four pillars of our existence.

What are some of the things that maybe done when you are held hostage by one of these emotions?

- Since we are made into emotional hostages by our thoughts, we will need to quiet the internal voice that is giving them power by practicing mental fasting. Choose specific periods of time every day where you stop all thought activity, and gradually increase the time frame. When thoughts come up, consciously do not grab on to them and say, "Pass." This will create a separation between the negative emotions and you, and eventually they will disappear as the desire to find other methods to permanently remove them becomes more appealing through EFT (Emotional Freedom Therapy), EMDR (Eye Movement Desensitization And Reprocessing), Time Line Therapy, and other counseling methods.

- Immobilize these thoughts for the time being until you can deal with them permanently. Acknowledge that they may appear to be real in your experience. However, they are not all of you, since you have many different qualities. Give them the lowest percentage that you find acceptable and compare them against all the good qualities that you can find within yourself. Use methods such as "The Works" by Byron Katie to understand their fallacy by saying, "Is it true?" "Is it really, really true?" "Where do I feel it in my body when I have them?" and "Who would I be if I did not have those thoughts?" Avoid using "do not," and use positive affirmations of what you want to be.

"Before the truth can set you free, you need to recognize which lie is holding you hostage." — RACHEL WOLCHIN

Freedom from Passive-Aggressive Behavior

By definition, passive-aggressive behavior is defined; "as the indirect expression of hostility, such as through procrastination, stubbornness, sullen behavior, or deliberate or repeated failure to accomplish requested tasks for which one is (often explicitly) responsible."

Why do people knowingly or unknowingly choose to have such behavior, what are its energetic roots, and what steps may be taken to neutralize such a desire? It is understood that the roots are the fear and avoidance of direct conflict led by the belief of being helpless and powerless.

In *Power vs. Force*, David Hawkins shows us that enlightenment passes through many layers up the emotional scale (the lowest emotions are, respectively; Shame, Guilt, Apathy, Grief, Fear, Desire, Anger, Pride, Courage, Neutrality before continuing as positive emotions). The energetic roots of passive-aggressive behavior emerge when individuals are trapped on the three levels of fear, desire, and anger. They anxiously try to move up to other levels to experience the bliss of the state of their peace with no success.

The prerequisite emotion of grief is followed by fear in order to find relief, and then continues to desire to pull out to the next emotional level of anger. Pride, the next level up, will be required to allow passage for processing emotions. The emotional stage of fear of losing whatever it is that may be important at the time will create the passive tendencies. The emotion of desire will pull them up out of fear to emotional state of anger, and they remain there exhibiting aggressive conduct.

A lot of people go through the emotional ladder without becoming chronic passive-aggressive individuals. The reason for developing a passive-aggressive attitude may be found in the next steps of emotional hierarchy, which are pride and then courage. Pride is required in order to pull us through the passive-aggressive vibration. Individuals who do not recognize their own greatness and do not understand that love is generated from within, as self to self without a need for other's approval, define themselves with limitations imposed by others, which leads to having low self-esteem. This low self-esteem translates into not having what may be known as the healthy type of pride independent from ego. Since pride and courage are not developed enough to properly transition the person to higher vibrations of joy and peace, the unprocessed emotion will find itself back at fear and anger again and again, as the individual becomes trapped by being passive-aggressive and repeating the same behavior.

Freedom, through a simple understanding of emotional ranking, will require temporarily inducing pride and courage until the behavior can be changed through more permanent practices. Further means of growth can be acquired to learn the power within until the internal infinite invincibility is recognized.

Practice the following as soon as signs of passive-aggressive responses are detected. Boost your pride by using a mantra and repeating to yourself how proud you are of yourself. Find any reason that you can find to enhance this quality at that moment. This will allow you to be confident and not worry about whatever it is that you fear. Also, it gives you the courage to express yourself and identify the specific subject without hiding behind the silence and false acceptance as you look for a win-win situation.

> "My friends, love is better than anger. Hope is better than fear. Optimism is better than despair. So let us be loving, hopeful, and optimistic. And we'll change the world." — JACK LAYTON

Habitual Thinking—Why Excuses?

When we really want to do something but we know it is not the right thing to do, we mischievously twist the truth to comfort ourselves by using an excuse. When Chico Marx's wife found him kissing the chorus girl, he said, "I was not kissing her, I was just whispering in her mouth."

Equally, when we do not want to do something that we consider not being important enough but somehow we feel obligated to do it, we again mischievously twist the truth to comfort ourselves by using an excuse.

However, the real truth is that usually the excuse is apparent to everyone else except the person using it. It is like the little child whose pants dropped in the mall. He was standing there naked, but he closed his eyes. His mom ran over there, pulled up his pants, and asked, "why did you close your eyes instead of pulling up your pants?" He responded, "I did not want anyone to see me naked."

Why do we use excuses? The excuse is a way of protecting some persona whose loss you fear will lessen who you believe yourself to be, so you must protect that persona at all costs, even if you have to create a misconception of the truth within yourself.

So, who would you be if you quiet down and are no longer the one they want you to be? Will you still use excuses to protect some idea that you may have of yourself that is not you and be bothered by the lies, or will you be totally free to move forward at lightning speed toward your goals?

How to Break the Chain of the Past

> *"The average person has about 60,000 thoughts per day, but the problem is that they are the same 60,000 thoughts they had yesterday."* — WAYNE DYER

Indeed, many of us get attached to the same defeating thoughts and have the same thoughts of yesterday over and over again. It seems that we get emotionally attached to them and very soon, like a chain, they anchor us to a place where we do not want to be, and they inhibit us from being free to move, expand, and be joyful.

It seems that we are afraid to break the chain and risk mourning the loss of the emptiness and the false comfort of the grounding force that the chain provided, even if it is attachment to something that is undesired.

Why can't we let go and transition to something more pleasing? The glue is the emotion. This emotion or energy in motion creates a bond between that event and the brain as the recordkeeper.

We have learned the desire to hold on in order to satisfy our insecurities. The solution to breaking the chain may be as simple as understanding that you were a vibrational match to what it was yesterday, and today you are a vibrational match to something different, new, and desirable.

The following steps may assist you in breaking the chain of the past:

- Separate yourself from your past by analyzing it from an outsider's view. Develop the understanding that individuals and circumstances of the past may have created certain experiences for you, but they did not create you. Remind yourself that you are love, you are loving, and you are beyond that and untouchable by all power outside of you other than the one that beats your heart.

- Stop living in the past and replace the times where you would usually refer to the past experiences with new desired experiences that are more pleasing to you.

- Meditate and find moments of mental fasting to stop the clusters of past memories from overpowering you.

- Try to fill yourself with new things that you desire and enjoy so the old experiences spill from your cup.

- Find ways to give up anxiety and rigidity and to be more courageous and flexible, to try new things and have more new experiences. As noted before, EMDR (Eye Movement Desensitization and Reprocessing), EFT (Emotional Freedom Therapy), Grief Therapy, and Time Line Therapy have shown to be very effective for making changes.

Mark Twain said, "Forgiveness is the fragrance that the violet sheds on the heel that has crushed it." Practice the following forgiveness meditations:

Method#1- (Forgiveness):

- Lay down or sit comfortably, with your back straight and supported

- Focus on your breathing. Let go of all other thoughts as you slowly breath in and out

- When ready, slowly breath in and out for one count

- Then, breath in and out for three counts, and hold an image of a person (living or passed) who you believe truly loves you, and who you love (this can also be an image of a spiritual being)

- Next, breath in and out for one count, and bring up the person or situation that you need to forgive, but superimpose the image of your loved one on top of it for this one count

- Then go back to breathing normally for one count and relax

- Repeat as needed and develop your personal experience from this helpful meditation

You will notice that your views of this person or situation starts changing, and eventually you will no longer be tormented by its unpleasant connection.

Method#2 - (Breaking the energetic cord):

- Lay down or sit comfortably with the intention to break the energetic tie to that one single event. This can be any disease that you may have or had or an actual undesired event that you may have had experienced.

- Think about that event and notice what part of your body that event is registered at and is being felt at.

- With your eyes closed, allow an imaginary cord to be extended from that part of your body to that person or that remote event. In case of a disease within your body, extend an imaginary cord from the part of your head that is related to that thought to the part of your body where the disease is being felt.

- Now, repeat quietly that you are sorry for anything that you may have done to cause this conflict.

- Follow up with stating that you forgive whatever harm that the other party has caused you.

- Imagine a sharp object that you can relate to such as a sharp scissor and cut the energetic cord as close to outside of your body as possible.

- Allow a healing white light to emerge from the cut surface to outside healing it. Allow a pink color ointment of light to heal and seal the wound that was caused by the cut cord.

Is It Yellow or Gold?

Most of us have experienced or witnessed discussions between friends, relatives, strangers, companions, spouses, colleagues, and others that start with enthusiasm, love, and positive energy. However, within a few rounds of back-and-forth discussion, it falls apart and gradually gets worse, ending with neither party giving up and going their separate ways in frustration and dissatisfaction.

It may start with something like this: "What a beautiful yellow flower." "Yes, it is beautiful, but it is more goldish than yellow." "But it is kind of yellow." "Well, it seems more gold to me." "Yellow." "Gold." "Yellow." "Gold." Then it continues to: "You never listen to me." "You always dismiss what I say." "You never care about what I think." And so on.

We provide different justifications for those circumstances, such as having a bad day, getting up the wrong side of the bed, not clicking with someone, not getting a good night's sleep, he or she is just that way, and many other excuses.

However, where is it coming from, how can it be detected early, and how can it be redirected to have a positive outcome? The answer may be found in this question. When asked, "What is the difference between a flower and a weed?" most people say that a flower is beautiful and a weed is less attractive. So, the answer is simple: judgment.

We always find what we look for. If we are truthful about our experiences, we can attest to the fact that when we look for good things in others, we always find it, and when we look for bad things, including being judgmental, we find that too.

Here are some energetic guidelines that can redirect your interactions to two different, opposite directions:

- Negatively impacting the outcome: Asking them to calm down, showing insincere empathy, telling them how they should be feeling, recommending what they should be doing under the circumstances, not allowing them to express their emotions by trying to dampen them, trying to force a resolution when it may be easier to not look for a winner and lovingly agree to drop it and to move on.

- Positively impacting the outcome: Expressing yourself fully, but in a kind and sincere way. Keep your voice low; it is most important to be calm, since it is the foundation for any self-defense, whether verbal or physical. Focus on making sentences that present niceness, take your time to be silent when things escalate, remind yourself that arguing is noise and not communication when you sense things going that direction, and try to create an opportunity to bring some level of laughter to the discussion. Remind yourself that discussion is about finding out what is right, while argument is about challenging who is right.

"To argue with a person who has renounced the use of reason is like administering medicine to the dead." — THOMAS PAINE

Regardless of all the reasons that our ego dictates for us to be right, personal happiness is only measured by each individual regardless of the surrounding environment. The old Chinese story says that "the student went to his master and said, 'Master, what is the secret to happiness?' He said, 'Not to argue with idiots.' The student said, 'Master, I completely disagree that this is it.' The master said, 'You are right.'"

Kindness

Have you ever thought about what kindness is and where it comes from? Many of us have learned to describe it as the opposite of being rude or hostile. Each of us may have a different definition to describe kindness in our own ways, however, there may be a universal description that will be conclusive of all.

Kindness is expressing love and compassion through our actions. Helping others without them needing to ask. Kindness brings resolution to a conflict when we give up interest in being right. It brings a rainbow to someone's cloud. Kindness is love in action without reasons and barriers produced by our left brain to convince us that there are no logical reasons to be kind without personal benefit. Kindness is that magical act that transforms everything for better; it breaks down the barriers and warms up our heart beyond interpretation of any language.

We are created with kindness as our universal default. It is impossible to find any infant that is unkind to himself, herself, or others. However, at one time or another we learn to be unkind in an attempt to protect ourselves from a physical or emotional threat, as fear teaches us to be unkind. This repeats itself as we grow up to be rude and exhibit hostile behavior.

Mostly, the threat is falsely interpreted on some misaligned assumption to protect the ego that we are less than some measuring bar that supposedly is considered to be whole. The mirage of believing that we are not whole drives us to be rude and hostile. The satisfaction of experiencing wholeness will bring us back to our kind roots. In this path of confusion and misunderstanding, we will never find wholeness and understanding, since our wholeness is independent from the ego and comes when we give up all measuring bars proposed by our limited left brain.

When we realize that wholeness requires the entire brain and cannot be possibly analyzed by a partial analytical mind, we find kindness. They say compassion is the glue that brings the right and left brain together as a whole. In a way, we act with kindness when we are compassionate. Once we find comfort in knowing the truth, that when people are rude they do not define you but reveal how afraid they are, we learn to be kind toward unkind people, since they need it most.

> *"Let no one ever come to you without leaving better and happier. Be the living expression of God's kindness: kindness in your face, kindness in your eyes, kindness in your smile."* — MOTHER TERESA

Studies have shown that in any act of kindness, the immune systems of the giver and receiver are equally strengthened. What is amazing to know is that even the immune system of the observer watching the act of kindness is raised by some level.

So how can we find more opportunities to be kind? We always find what we look for. To be kind requires making a conscious decision to be kind by removing all the barriers that have been reprogrammed to be unkind.

> *"Be kind whenever possible. It is always possible."* — DALAI LAMA

Me, Myself, and I

The question of who you are may start with a simple inquiry of self by asking, who was the little infant who began to crawl? Who was the little boy or girl who ran everywhere, playing and being mischievous? Who was the young teenager who saw the world as the enemy or fell in love with every glance? Who was the one who had all the dreams of being and doing to change the world? Who was the one who did all the foolish things or made many mistakes? Who was the one who accomplished the impossible and failed some? Who was the old man who took comfort in being quiet to see the world passing by, or the old woman who just wanted to tell her stories quietly? Who is the formless being who no longer is?

The answer to all of them is me, myself, and I . . . or maybe not, maybe there is something else.

All the historical documents based on the ones before us have told us in different forms that there may be something else. *The Bhagavad Gita*, Rumi, Buddha, Moses, Socrates, Jesus, Confucius, and many other sources have told us in their own ways that there is something more.

Moses, when questioning the burning bush at Mount Sinai, was told that "I am that I am" is the authority. Rumi profoundly refers to this "I am that I am" as the ocean, and to a drop of this ocean that beats each of our hearts as the ocean in a drop.

"Me, myself, and I" is the powerless portion of this "I am that I am," yet we have the illusion that it is all we are. *A Course in Miracles* states that "if you knew who walks beside you at all times, you would never experience fear and doubt again."

The institute for the investigation of miracles tells us of thousands of miracles that show evidence of this unlimited authority beyond the limited version of our belief. Who is that authority who interferes at the last moment to change the direction of our actions when we have exhausted our capacity of "me, myself, and I" to be powerless?

What causes a woman who is about to commit suicide to decide to write a suicide note just before she shoots herself? In the middle of her note, the desire to call her pastor arises with the recollection of a phone number that she thinks is his.

She calls and he answers, but he is shocked that she had found him. What had caused the woman to find his number when he is two thousand miles away on his vacation away from his office? For some reason, his family had gone to the store and he had decided to stand outside near a public phone with the number that she has found access to call into just at the moment that she needed it.

Most of us can attest to the fact that there is a driver behind the scenes. It is that ageless being that observes all the questions that were raised at the beginning. It is that "I am that I am" that gives us all the power when we recognize that "me, myself, and I" are not what we truly are.

In *Journey of Souls*, Michael Newton explains that all his subjects under hypnosis had pointed out the fact that we only have physical experiences with a portion of ourselves, while our other energetic portion always stays connected and observes and guides and interferes so we are never alone.

So let's ask this question again: Who are you? If you see the world as limited, cold, unfriendly, hateful, disconnected, lonely, sad, and angry, then your answer is me, myself, and I, since those are the byproducts of limitations.

And if you see the world as loving, friendly, unified, happy, joyful, and compassionate, then your answer shows your connection and awareness of who you truly are by recognizing and trusting that "I am that I am."

Our power comes from our choice to align ourselves with that energy that flows with the Universe's flow of peace and joy or to oppose it, Simply said, it may be summarized in the story of the earlier chapter for the little boy who went to his grandfather and said, "Grandfather, it seems that there are two wolves inside me. One is good and the other one is bad. Which one will win?" His grandfather said, "The one that you will feed most."

Ordinary or Extraordinary?

The word "Ordinary" has been defined as "with no special or distinctive features; normal, usual, standard, typical, common." The word "extraordinary" has been defined as "exceptional, amazing, stunning, incredible, unbelievable, outstanding, unforgettable, unique, noteworthy."

The misconception begins when we start finding ways to be extraordinary to feel worthy. Very soon our self-worth is shifted to the extraordinary in order to value ourselves, and eventually the ordinary becomes something that seems lacking and deficient in some ways.

Not sure where it all began, but its fallacy is beyond humorous, as we force ourselves and our children to be extraordinary at all times and in everything we do in order to qualify ourselves as successful.

However, there is a different view that explains it all in harmony. To be ordinary is our default state of being in complete joy, peace, and perfection, without superiority or inferiority. Sometimes we choose to be extraordinary when we are inspired and desire to experience something different and without superiority or inferiority, just as before, but for the enjoyment of the experience. It is like going hiking and enjoying the hike on a nice sunny day, or when you choose to have a different experience of flying for a few hours and do some hang gliding along the way. Each experience has its own value without being superior or inferior to the other one.

Assuming that the above is understood, the next question would be, how do we get to be extraordinary?

If you want to be ordinary, investigate what is happening and If you want to be extraordinary, investigate what is not happening. It seems that our virtue starts when we are not aware of something or simply do not know. Once we know it, we do two things. We either take action or we do nothing. This does not necessarily mean physical action; it could be just a thought as an action, or being silent with no thought about it as inaction.

Nevertheless, we are accustomed to analyzing all our movements by the actions that we take as the only important part of this measuring bar. Consequently, we do not put any emphasis or value on the time that we remain silent, considering it nonexistence. Similarly, we recognize and are preoccupied with the state of our health by investigating the rhythm and sound of our heartbeats, while the part that is silent and the gap that exists between the two heartbeats does not get as much recognition. It is given that it exists, but it seems to have no value.

Historically, the most extraordinary generals, scientists, philosophers, teachers, pioneers, leaders, attorneys, politicians, and businesspeople react otherwise. They tend to investigate and analyze what is not happening in order to excel and succeed, to reach the levels that we qualify as extraordinary.

Our misconception may be that extraordinary people are ordinary people who are acting in some extra way above what is expected of them. However, the extraordinary part comes from recognizing the importance of not doing things at the right time. It is the way of extraordinary people to value silence as the extra step to make all that may be considered impossible by some into possibility.

> *"The window is the absence of the wall, and it gives air and light because it is empty. Be empty of all mental content, of all imagination and effort, and the very absence of obstacles will cause reality to rush in."* — SRI NISARGADATTA MAHARAJ

Science, Health, and Miracles

We are grateful to science and all scientists for their true, genuine dedication for investigating diseases in attempts to find a cure, so that humanity will not perish during the times that they may have forgotten the true universal power of their self-healing abilities.

However, science will never find health, simply because health comes from the English word meaning "whole," and science mainly comes from left analytical brain, which is only half of the brain. It is impossible to find and comprehend wholeness with something that is not generated from that view.

If ease is our interpretation of the awareness with its related feelings, emotional sensations, and its byproducts leading to love, joy, and peace, then lack of this awareness will be our interpretation of the opposite—disease, commonly known as disease.

Dis-ease does not exist in energy since energy only flows, transforms, and changes phases as laws of thermodynamics promise their validity. Therefore, it is impossible to have lack of ease or dis-ease in our energy field. Consequently, if we are about 99.99 percent energy and less than 0.01 percent mass, then why do we experience disease?

The answer is the power and ability of our focus versus the level of its clarity and its contamination to believe that there is something lacking in our process of creation. This may also be called our belief. However, if it is just the matter of having a certain belief that has no doubt imbedded in it, then how can we explain someone experiencing a disease when they are not even aware of it and have no focus on experiencing such a disease?

The universe has no agenda as to what form of dis-ease falls under what category. If the belief is associated with "lack," then all its byproducts in all the categories and subcategories fall under "dis-ease," versus its intended complete version of "ease."

The best way to describe this is through the thousands of people who have shared their near-death experiences with the rest of the humanity but have not been understood. Or, those who have had direct experiences of instantaneous healing through miracles, when their focus on the lack shifted to recognizing their perfection as their disease moves to a healing state of ease within seconds, to science's amazement. Many of the organizations investigating the authenticity of these miracles always close their reports by stating that some extraordinary event had taken place. In actuality, and from the universe's point of view, those are just ordinary states of our being that we had forgotten about but are reminded of in rare occasions through near-death experiences and miracles.

Imagine this: You have been to the ocean and you know how beautiful, powerful, and great it is. You tell everyone else about it, but they have only seen small ponds in their neighborhood, so they cannot believe you. Finally, one of them says, "Please give me directions, since I really want to see it." You give them specific directions to go down this highway, that byway, to turn at this road and that road, and to finally make the last turn as you arrive by the ocean.

You wait anxiously, knowing what an amazing experience this will be, and finally call the person to rejoice in and celebrate this amazing state of knowing with his direct experience of seeing the ocean. To your amazement, he says, "I have been waiting here for a long time. I followed your directions very carefully, and I am exactly at the spot that you had directed me, but I do not see any ocean." You keep explaining that it is beautiful and it is powerful and it is the absolute truth, but you keep hearing back that there is no ocean there.

Finally, you review the directions step by step with him and realize that he is right and he is exactly at the location where he is supposed to be. Then you ask, "Do you hear the ocean? Can you smell the water even though you do not see it?"

He impatiently says, "Yes, yes, I do." You say. "Just follow those hints and see where it takes you."

Suddenly, you hear a cry of joy and bliss that screams, "IT IS A MIRACLE. I can see how beautiful and magnificent it is, exactly as you had said. All this time, it was behind me and I was looking at the opposite direction. All I had to do was to turn around to see and to recognize its magnificence."

Solution or Problem?

Every time a problem arises, a solution arises too. Our power comes from the ability of our choice to be able to put our attention and focus on the solution or on the problem. We can act powerless and waste our resources further on the problem or be powerful by maximizing our energy as we look for a solution.

First, we must understand how we define what a problem is and how it is initiated before we can evaluate what needs to develop next.

A "problem" is defined as whatever that is opposing what is desired. Since what is desired will mean something different to each person, what is considered to be a problem by one may not be interpreted that way by others.

An obstacle on the way to succeed may be defined by one person as a problem, while interpreted by another as the solution to develop skills to prepare his or her path toward another desired task that, without development of that skill, would have been impossible to achieve.

Regardless of how we define a problem, any effort and attention given to it more than for identification and evaluation purposes is a waste of our resources.

So how do we prepare and implement this shift of energy? Interestingly enough, when our attitude is to be a problem finder, we find problems at every corner and at each transaction. Equally, when our attitude is to be a solution finder, we become overwhelmed by the number of options presenting themselves from an angle that was never apparent before. We must shift ourselves to see the same situation from a different view to be able to discover the solution.

When we are inspired, meaning being in spirit, we fly toward our desired goals and are not distracted by anything that may be opposing them. When we are not, we push ourselves to crawl where all the bumps on the road present themselves as problems.

Peaceful warriors of the Shaolin Monastery can attest to this fact. Through martial arts, their weapon training is not to be offensive, but historically has been practiced by learning all that is needed about a weapon so they can defend themselves and others against it when it is used by the aggressors. They are never focused on the weapon alone to the point that they become demobilized, forgetting about all the other skills, methods, and weapons that they have available.

Similarly, focusing on a problem for any reason other than learning how to defend against it will be counterproductive to our path to succeed in what we desire.

When you let go of the fear of being powerless to focus on the problem, and are empowered to recognize your true capabilities, the solution will amazingly appear. Einstein said, "The intellect has little to do on the road to discovery. There comes a leap in consciousness, call it intuition or what you will, and the solution comes to you and you don't know how or why."

The Anatomy of a Lie

Is there such a thing as a white lie or other lies based on our personal measurements and level of honesty? Or maybe a lie is just a lie, and a deception is far from the truth regardless of what we call it and the circumstances leading to it. Sometimes we are fearful and speak the "lie"; sometimes we should tell the truth but hold back quietly; sometimes we know we cannot make a promise and still make it; and there are many more versions of lying that we have become accustom to.

Let's examine the need to lie. We lie when we are afraid that the truth will have some significant unsatisfactory result directed at us; or, sometimes in case of a white lie, we believe we are protecting others. Fear exists only in response to a desire to protect something whose loss we believe will diminish our wholeness. So, in order to examine the reasons to lie, we need to investigate what it is that we are trying to protect. Additionally, we need to recognize that our wholeness and perfection does not need protection to begin with, since it is independent from opinions of others and not subject to any threats.

One of my favorite stories is when Jesus took a fig from a fig tree on the Sabbath, and his disciples told him that he should not eat on Sabbath. He explained to them that what goes into the mouth is not important because it goes through the body and gets discharged; instead, what comes out of our mouths, such as lies, deception, and hurtful words, is much more important because it comes from our heart and shows who we truly are inside.

Different studies have shown that our body gestures, blinking, and eye positions change when we lie. They have documented that lying makes our heart race, makes us pant, increases our blood pressure and sweat levels, and causes our muscles to weaken. These are signs of the body experiencing stress.

Basically, we are designed to go downstream, like rafting down the river, when we are loving, joyful, honest, and compassionate, since that is the universe's natural flow of energy. We go upstream when we lie and are dishonest, exposing ourselves to extra stress, friction, and inefficiency, requiring more energetic resources. The most destructive people in our history used lying as their main strategy to succeed and become oppressors, such as Hitler, who said, "Make the lie big, make it simple, keep saying it, and eventually they will believe it."

"For every good reason there is to lie, there is a better reason to tell the truth." — BO BENNETT

Examine your priorities and you will find the right response only when you act independent from your "need" and are driven by your love and compassion.

It's easy to get sidetracked, on the narrow Way . . . with so many distractions, getting thrown at us each day.

It's easy to get off course, when following the Light . . . with so many diversions, being shoved in our sight.

It's easy to lose focus, when trying to live the Life . . . with so many disturbances, causing us conflict and strife.

It's easy to lose sight of, the straight, narrow gate . . . with so many differences, throwing us off our gait.

It's easy to be diverted, from the Light, Life and the Way, but, we can be redirected . . . to the Truth ~

if we stop and pray!

— DEBORAH ANN

The Art of De-memorizing

One of our biggest gifts is our ability to memorize things. We also have another gift that does not get practiced nor recognized as often, which is the ability to de-memorize.

We have an unlimited potential and capability to store the events of our lives and our experiences. This is an amazing gift and superbly efficient way of carrying these experiences as we memorize them to be recalled at will. However, when these memories are considered unpleasant, keeping and recalling them controlled at will or uncontrolled is no longer beneficial to our well-being. Once the lesson is learned, repetitive recall of these memories no longer serves any universal purpose.

In order to understand the art of de-memorizing, we must first comprehend the act of memorizing. We memorize things by committing them to our memory to be stored and to be recalled. These things are information, experiences, facts, figures, data, pictures, and stories that are witnessed and experienced voluntarily or involuntarily, but recorded the same in our memory banks.

The interdisciplinary link between cognitive psychology and neuroscience tells us that the memory is a part of cognitive neuroscience. This begins at our early childhood, at about three years old, and includes all forms of our memory: short term, long term, working memory, and autobiographical memory.

Most of us have a misconception that our power comes from our thoughts. Our self-absorbed ego demands that nothing else exists other than this body. Therefore, brain activity is at the root of our power, and rightfully so, as the ego's function is to protect the body.

However, our whole being recognizes that we are spiritual beings having physical ego experiences for this temporary period. With this knowledge, we recognize our true power that stems from the silent gap between the two thoughts that can initiate and choose physical thoughts.

Our power comes from choosing to memorize thought A as we de-memorize thought B. This power chooses to make the thought A dominant as it silences thought B. In a way, we choose to memorize and de-memorize through this power.

Simply said, by giving attention and directing our focus to thought A for what is desired, we can de-memorize the thought B, which may be undesirable. However, the remnants of de-memorized thoughts remain in our system and are stored deep in our subconscious level.

A computer that is bombarded by spam and viruses has been designed with a feature to clear and restore it back to its original conditions through the reset button. The only thing required is the ability to detect its conditions and the operator's willingness to push the reset button.

We have been equipped with such a reset button that can clear all the de-memorized thoughts that may be counterproductive to our state of well-being and bombard us with what may not be conducive to our universal state of joy and well-being. This reset button is called forgiveness. The only thing that it requires is the operator's willingness to reach for it and apply it.

Still, for those whose mischievous minds demand a physical exercise to de-memorize a thought, there is a method that can be used:

- Find a quiet place to clear your mind without interruptions or disturbance of the outside world.

- Close your eyes and bring your attention to what needs to be de-memorized.

- Notice its shape, color, and any identifying name associated with it.

- It appears that it has an invisible boundary. Define it!

- Now rotate this boundary as fast as you can in a counterclockwise rotation.

- Try it several times as needed, and you will notice that its intensity reduces and that the thought eventually vanishes as you begin to discover your ability to de-memorize.

The Attitude of "What Is Wrong"

In the privacy of your own mind and without any desire to defend yourself, look into this question about your attitude toward how you approach all the events of your life. Do you search for what is wrong all the time, or are you mostly satisfied as you approach your daily life's events?

The attitude that searches for what is wrong is never disappointed, as it finds all the reasons to fulfill that question and ignores all the opposing reasons and justifications. Equally, the attitude of "what is right?" will find all the motives supporting unlimited justifications of why it is right with all the certainty.

They say that when Mother Teresa was walking in the villages with all the filth, poverty, sickness, and wars around her, she would stop and would point out to a little green leaf that was left in the middle of all other dried up vegetation to appreciate its beauty.

The attitude of "what is right" is far from the attitude of "what is wrong," as both look at the same event, but one sees beauty, health, prosperity, courage, and love, where the other sees ugliness, sickness, poverty, weakness, and fear.

The attitude of "what is wrong" stems from the belief that something is missing and is inadequate. The attitude of "what is right" stems from the belief that there is a personal satisfaction among all parts of the individual (me, myself, and I) with no inadequacy that needs to be filled to create the missing part. Both of these attitudes are byproducts of how we view ourselves and are equally available to us, pending our choices and impacting the outcome of the same events and experiences with opposite results.

We never engage in a physical act of walking into a store intending to look for "what is missing." We always have the attitude of looking for something specific that we desire, and when we do not find what we are looking for, we continue going to other stores until we find what we are exactly looking for. However, when we approach the events of our lives with the attitude of "what is wrong," in reality we are searching for something that we believe is already missing and that cannot be found.

The byproducts of missing things are always like swimming upstream, experiencing resistance and dissatisfaction.

Since a thought is like the tip of an arrow that gives direction to our energetic being to reach our desired target, it is important that we direct it to what is desired and not what is missing and wrong, in order to change our attitude from "what is wrong" to "what is right." Pick a signal to remind yourself, when you notice you are looking for "what is wrong," as the tool to redirect your thoughts to search for what is right. Practice it as often as possible. (For example, snap your finger or slap your hand to remind yourself every time you detect that a change of attitude in your thinking is needed.)

"When you stop chasing the wrong things, you give the right things a chance to catch you." — LOLLY DASKAL

"You don't have to be great to start, but you have to start to be great." — ZIG ZIGLAR

The Cookie Thief

How often do we feel hurt or get upset thinking that we have been mistreated and wronged by others? We act as judge and jury to conclude that there was a huge agenda and conspiracy behind everything that occurred based on that person and the universe collaborating to hurt us and prevent us from being successful or achieving what we desire.

In her masterful program "The Work," Byron Katie sums it all up by offering the first two questions of the four steps, these two simple yet common misconceptions of the brain memes: "Is it true?" and followed by "Is it really, really true?". How often do we find ourselves making a decision based on false interpretations of our views regarding something far removed from reality, and yet we believe in its absolute certainty?

We are the interpreter of our experiences, and no brain surgeon has ever been able to see a "thought," and no scientist has ever been able to identify "not having the rent money, family stress, relationship issues, health challenges" in beta-level activities of a brain scan other than the fact that during beta-level activities, our body experiences stress.

So the interpreter has a huge role in the outcome and the events that follow an interpretation, since once decided, that outcome will dictate to the body what emotion to experience, which will put our body into joy, increasing our immune system and creating good feelings, or the opposite, which will increase stress and make us sad.

One of my favorite stories that reminds us of how wrong we can be without realizing it, is the beautiful Valerie Cox poem called "The Cookie Thief":

> A woman was waiting at an airport one night, with several long hours before her flight. She hunted for a book in the airport shops, bought a bag of cookies and found a place to drop.
>
> She was engrossed in her book but happened to see, that the man sitting beside her, as bold as could be . . . grabbed a cookie or two from the bag in between, which she tried to ignore to avoid a scene.
>
> So, she munched the cookies and watched the clock, as the gutsy cookie thief diminished her stock. She was getting more irritated as the minutes ticked by, thinking, "If I wasn't so nice, I would blacken his eye."

With each cookie she took, he took one too, when only one was left, she wondered what he would do. With a smile on his face, and a nervous laugh, he took the last cookie and broke it in half.

He offered her half, as he ate the other, she snatched it from him and thought, ". . . Oooh, brother. This guy has some nerve and he's also rude, why he didn't even show any gratitude!"

She had never known when she had been so galled, and sighed with relief when her flight was called. She gathered her belongings and headed to the gate, refusing to look back at the thieving ingrate.

She boarded the plane, and sank in her seat, then she sought her book, which was almost complete. As she reached in her baggage, she gasped with surprise; there was her bag of cookies, in front of her eyes.

"If mine are here," she moaned in despair, "the others were his, and he tried to share." Too late to apologize, she realized with grief, that she was the rude one, the ingrate, the thief.

The Illusion of Our Perception

How big is a problem when we perceive it to be one? When someone says, "I have an issue," what does that mean, and how critical or insignificant is it? *A Course in Miracles* says, "You have no issues, you only think you do."

If you are hypnotized and told that there is a chair in the middle of your living room where none else sees it, you will be the only one walking around it all your life, avoiding it until you are awakened from that hypnotic stage.

What appears to be your reality may not be perceived as absolute reality. As an observer of your life, you are the same child who was five years old; you are the same person who was ten years old; twenty, thirty, forty, and more in your past, and you will be the same one who will observe it in the future, with or without your body.

What would be the perception of a human who lives one hundred years compared to an insect who lives three days? From the human's perspective, it is a very short three days. From the insect's perception, it is all he knows to be a very long life, equating to one hundred years.

Therefore, the observer's perception measures it all. There is no scientific proof that the problems that we define as issues ever exist. All the brain measurement studies have been unable to show anything that we define as problems other than acknowledging that the frequency of the brain activity increases during beta levels, when we deal with nonloving thoughts.

People are constantly tormented by many issues and seek relief from them; others provide compassion and assistance to relieve them of their issues. However, those issues can also disappear when the observer defining them as a problem ceases that perception and views them from a different angle. This is same as waking up from a hypnotic stage, when the subject realizes that there was never a chair in the living room to begin with.

How can we train ourselves to not be fooled by the illusion of perception that is not the universal default or the absolute truth? The illusion that makes us believe that we have issues interrupts our peace, joy, and happiness, leading to sorrow and pain.

On average, we blink twenty-five times per minute. That means that we have twenty-five opportunities in every minute to look at the same situation differently. Scientists have told us that the limited angle of 1 degree of our eyes as view ports are continued to be filled with images via our brain's pre-programming. we see what our brain chooses to fill in the blanks with based on our perception of what is desired to be seen.

So, with this new understanding, question the authority of what you perceive to be an "issue." View it from a different angle with the knowledge that things will change once you choose to change how you look at them. Allow yourself to view things from the universe's absolute perception of being fearless, where unconditional love, compassion, and kindness are the only reality.

> *"Everything that irritates us about others can lead us to*
> *an understanding of ourselves." —* CARL JUNG

The Love or the Loveless?

It is impossible for the loveless to find love because it is impossible to give away something that we do not have.

Language is a very poor interpreter for defining internal explorations and assigning words to them. We are at the mercy of the ear that hears those words and their internal interpretations, hoping that they will find the same meaning.

So love is one of the words that is defined daily by multitudes and assumed to mean the same for all, but each has unique interpretations for oneself.

Love is the absence of loveless. It is going downstream with the flow of the universe. Abraham Maslow said, "One of man's greatest needs is the feeling of belonging and love." We are loving when we feel that we belong and are accepted by all our physiological interactions and by all that we come in contact with.

This ease of flow going downstream is smoother, softer, and easier than the upstream flow. Its counterpart is interpreted to be the up flow resistance. Our definition of this ease is "love" and all opposing it is "loveless."

Love, according to Plato and Aristotle, may be summarized in the following seven types:

1. Sexual or passionate love that is the construct of most romantic love, based on the process of striving for survival and reproduction.

2. Friendship love that is shared goodwill based on being useful; being pleasant; and being good, that is, rational and virtuous leading to companionship, dependability, and trust.

3. Familial love that is the love between parents and their children with fondness based on familiarity or dependency independent from personal qualities.

4. Universal love, such as the love for strangers, nature, or God, which is unselfish for the welfare of others. It leaves us with an elevated feeling associated with better mental and physical health, along with longevity. It also reciprocates with gifts and favors that may be of much greater value. It helps us to build and maintain the psychological, social, and environmental fabric that shields, sustains, and enriches us.

5. The playful or uncommitted love. It can involve activities such as teasing and dancing, or more overt flirting, seducing, and conjugating. The focus is on fun, and sometimes also on conquest, with no strings attached to be casual, undemanding, and uncomplicated, and can be very long-lasting.

6. Practical love founded on reason or duty and one's longer-term interests. Sexual attraction diminishes in favor of personal qualities and compatibilities, shared goals, and making it work.

7. Self-love, which can be healthy or unhealthy. Unhealthy self-love with inflated sense of one's status, abilities, or accomplishments, especially when accompanied by arrogance. It may disregard truth and may promote injustice, conflict, and enmity. Or, healthy self-love, which is our cognitive, self-esteem, and emotional appraisal of our own worth relative to that of others. It is the foundation through which we think, feel, and act as it reflects and determines our relation to ourselves, to others, and to the world. However, it is possible to be highly self-confident and yet to have very low self-esteem.

Rumi said:

> "What is poison? Anything which is more than our necessity is poison. It may be Power, Wealth, Hunger, Ego, Greed, Laziness, Love, Ambition, Hate or anything.
>
> What is fear? Non-acceptance of uncertainty. If we accept that uncertainty, it becomes adventure.
>
> What is envy? Non-acceptance of Good in others. If we accept that good, it becomes Inspiration.
>
> What is anger? Non-acceptance of things which are beyond our control. If we accept, it becomes Tolerance.
>
> What is hatred? Non-acceptance of person as he is. If we accept the person unconditionally, it becomes Love."

The Gift of "Broken"!

Something amazing happens when we are broken, regardless of what the cause may be.

Being broken means that we believe somehow that something or someone has damaged us to the point that we need to be fixed. It means that we have been worn down to a state that we can no longer fight the conditions. A Heart attack may be nothing other than a heart that has been emotionally broken many times, leading to a "broken heart."

History has shown that every quantum leap of our progression toward a change was led by an individual who had some form of broken story.

The 13th. Century Persian poet and philosopher, Rumi said, "Maybe you are searching among the branches for what only appears in the roots."

The butterfly transitioning from a caterpillar has two distinct states. One is living in a shell as a caterpillar and the other one is the state of flying as a butterfly. To transition from the dense state of a shell to levitating toward the weightless state of flying as a butterfly requires a quantum leap beyond the familiar state of what is.

The butterfly never thinks that something is broken because it is not flying yet. The universe has no concept of inadequacy leading to be broken. It only transforms from one state to the other with its universal default: that all is well, all has always been well, and all will always be well regardless of the observer's understanding of its concept.

Buddha said that we are here to experience suffering until we realize that suffering is not needed (paraphrased).

So why do we experience being broken, and how can we learn to understand its anatomy? It is unconscionable to tell someone who has reasons to believe that he or she has been broken, due to some event or by someone, that the universe had intended for he or she to experience that.

However, nothing seems as it appears, and the only answer may lie in the roots and not the branches, as Rumi had noted. The energetic universe only flows by polarity of energy, as we have been given the choice of "free will" to be a part of this energetic expansion to enjoy our creativity. The "choice" is to create as we flow with this energy, or to oppose it.

These choices must be evaluated independent from time to represent the roots, otherwise each lifetime experience only reflects the branches, leading to misinterpretation of being broken. We cannot understand a book by only reading one chapter of it. Removing time and our perception of its +/-100 years from human's life span limitation allows us to see the book in its entirety beyond this one chapter of our present experiences.

Regardless of philosophical views of the interpretations relating to being broken, the relief may be provided for the one who is experiencing it with the power of emotions, by cutting the emotional energetic cords per these steps:

1. Sit or lay down quietly with the intention of cutting the energetic cord to a specific event.

   (Note: This also can be done for a disease or discomfort within your body to cut the cord between the part of brain that is holding that event and that organ.)

2. Bring up the event and notice where in your body it is being sensed.

3. Draw an energetic cord from the center of that part of your body to that event or person.

4. Now quietly say that you are sorry for whatever it is that you may have done toward that situation, issue or person.

5. Then follow up by saying that you forgive whatever that event or person may have caused you.

6. Continue by cutting the energetic cord close to your body via a sharp object that you can imagine, like scissors.

7. Allow a continuous white light to project out from your body to the universe through the point that you had cut the cord as it begins to heal it.

8. Now, apply a pink energetic ointment to the hole where the cord was cut to heal and seal it at your body.

"The secret to change is to focus all of your energy, not on fighting the old, but on building the new." — SOCRATES

The Hierarchy of EGO!

What would God, the source, the creator, the absolute, the universe respond to all faces of the hierarchy of the EGO (Earthly Guided Only) for gender, color, attractiveness, money, physical criteria, and all its other faces?

Einstein said, "All I want is to be able to think like God does." So let's think like God does for a moment and view the above question from an absolute universal point of view.

To see everything through God's point of view, we must view it from the energetic side of us, since we are 99.9% energy.

That energy in physical terms is converted to have electrical essence as voltage and electrical current through our body's foundation, our cells.

If the universal intention had any concept for the hierarchy of one being higher, resulting in having more resources, then that would mean that the one with higher status must receive more energy.

What does this translate to? We all get the same amount of energy from the universe, showing to be about -25 mv across our cells in order to have an alkaline pH environment of 7.45. Any more or less of this energy will lead to emotional and physical illnesses and eventually death of the physical body.

It is safe to assume that the source that created it all, regardless of what name is used to identify it, never intended for any hierarchy due to the above-mentioned, since it provides equal energy without partiality to all its creations. This energy only gets interrupted when as individuals we choose to block its path.

The universal intention for this equal energy is to create all that we desire without attachments to its outcome. There is nothing more enjoyable than running toward our desired goals and to excel and succeed in accomplishing what is intended without attachments to that outcome. This means to help others on this path, recognizing that their path is parallel, and wishing them to succeed as we do. Only then we can see the world as was intended without the EGO's lens of judgment with joy, peace, compassion, and its byproduct of wholeness of perfect health.

Mike Dooley through his book *The Top Ten Things Dead People Want to Tell You* and many other investigations for near death experience (NDE) patients have shown that the hierarchy of EGO-driven criteria does not exist from the universal point of view. All of what we consider to be the grading of our relationships with material things and others, including ourselves, disappear in absence of judgment when viewed without fear of loss of attachments. We recognize equal beauty for the bush and the flower only without judgment.

Since the pearl is inside and all answers are hidden within that silent voice inside, all we need is to quiet down and stop being distracted by the noise of the empty drummers who promote fear. Fearless living is not courage, fighting for peace is not peaceful living, fighting the disease is not perfect health, fighting poverty is far from prosperity. We must use all our resources, our energy, toward what needs to be promoted and must not reduce it for what is not desired. Only then we recognize that the universe has unlimited resources when we all act as one, and only then the hierarchy of the EGO will cease to exist.

> "Yesterday I was clever, so I wanted to change the world.
> Today I am wise, so I am changing myself." — RUMI

The Message to Garcia

During Spanish–American War, the president needed to give important specific directions to the leader of the insurgents. García was hiding deep in the jungle and mountains in an unknown location in Cuba. It was urgent that he was contacted to follow the specific directions; the outcome of the war depended on this message.

The concern was, how could this time-sensitive message be delivered under all the undesirable, nearly impossible conditions?

The president was notified that if anyone could do this, would be a man named Rowan. Rowan was given the sealed letter. After four days he landed in Cuba. After three weeks he had passed through the jungle and had exited the other side after successfully delivering the letter to García.

We always find what we look for and where we put our focus and attention. When we look for understanding, we find it, and when we look for misunderstanding, we find that too. When we look for love, we find it, and we look for lack of it, we succeed in finding that too. When we look for perfect health, we find it, and when we look for not being sick, we equally find sickness too.

Rowan never asked, "Who is García? Where is he? How can I find him? Where should I go? How can I get back after I am done? What if I do not make it? What if I fail?" He was given the message, and he saw himself delivering the message and being back where he wanted to be. The rest was just details. The bump on the road never stops us from going to the party other than momentarily slowing us down to get over the bump.

The first law of thermodynamic tells us that it is impossible for energy to die. It can only change phase. This means that once you have a thought and it is focused toward the direction of your goal, it cannot die and it must be accomplished. The only way it can be changed is when you willingly redirect it to something different to change its phase. We have a misconception that some of our goals may be impossible, as we fall short of reaching them. This illusion may become easily apparent when we change the lens of how we view things, as it magically changes from "impossible" to "I'm possible."

We all set goals and with all sincerity and determination try to reach them. However, there is that unspoken internal attitude and belief that at the end will determine and will ensure their fulfillments or lack of them. Even "ask and be given" and "knock and the door will be opened" continue by giving us the technology to fulfill them by stating that "ask without hidden motives and surround yourself by your asking so your joyfulness will be full."

Among many documented reports of potential miracles, there is one that may exemplify the power of our asking. The woman who has been waiting and planning to be her best friend's maid of honor, and who has special messages for the bride on the wedding day, happens to come down with severe cold and fever. She is disappointed to tell her friend that she is not able to get out of bed to the wedding as her mother nurses her. She has been crying out with all her power to the universe to provide an opportunity for her to attend the wedding. Finally, shortly before the wedding, she hears a voice inside her room that says, "Be still to be healed." She does so, and to her surprise, a glowing spark of energy appears in front of her and touches her on each shoulder. Instantly her cold and fever are gone, and she is able to attend the wedding. However, her fever and cold return as soon as she gets back home, because she was not clear in her asking about perfect health, but was specific about being healthy enough to attend the wedding. Amazingly, the universe always delivers with perfection and clarity what we energetically ask for, independent from any form of language, whether spoken or thought.

So what are you looking for when you have a desire? Will you be thinking of all the reasons that you cannot have it, or like the message to García, will you deliver the message to the universe that it is already done as you await its details to physically present themselves in your life? The choice is yours, and both options are equally available!

The Mystery of "Self-Esteem"!

Self-esteem simply means an estimate of our self-worth or the outcome of our self-estimate. It is how we view ourselves and how we estimate our self-worth against a given criteria.

Most of us have a misconception that the base for self-evaluation we compare ourselves to is universal and is constant. However, this mirage has conceptual fallacy, since it is totally driven by each individual's focus.

Each soul at its energetic conception is created with complete perfection, meaning that it has perfect alignment with its energetic source to have 100% self-esteem. This self-esteem has no inadequacy. This pure energetic soul becomes exposed to the vibration of the womb and its surroundings as time passes. The efficiency of this self-esteem remains at 100% or reduces based on these early vibrational exposures. Once the baby is born and becomes more exposed to society and different measuring bars via his or her brain activities, the self-esteem starts taking shape and compares itself to the bases that the individual has focused on to be the criteria.

The simple universal law that always applies remains to be the absolute truth and the constant: we are born with 100% self-esteem and we die with 100% self-esteem. Any view of this to be any less stems from the fallacy of our focus that some selected criteria has been given values that cannot be reached.

Simply said, our interpretation of our wholeness comes from 100% self-esteem. Once we find a hole in our wholeness, this self-esteem is reduced and lacking. We find ourselves less than whole: incomplete, inadequate, incompetent, and unsatisfied. This is the beginning of our search to be confident, looking for its byproducts of happiness, joy, and peace that once we knew as a child.

Maslow's expanded hierarchy of needs has pioneered the steps for many human behaviors including our self-esteem:

Biological and physiological needs (air, food, drink, shelter, etc.)

Safety needs (protection, security, etc.).

Love and belongingness needs (friendship, intimacy, trust, and acceptance, etc.).

Esteem needs:

Esteem for oneself (dignity, achievement, mastery, independence, etc.)

Esteem from others; the desire for reputation or respect (status, prestige, etc.)

Cognitive needs (knowledge, understanding, curiosity, exploration, need for meaning and predictability)

Aesthetic needs (appreciation and search for beauty, balance, form, etc.)

Self-actualization needs (realizing personal potential, self-fulfillment, seeking personal growth and peak experiences)

Transcendence needs (A person is motivated by values that transcend beyond the personal self; e.g. mystical experiences and certain experiences with nature, aesthetic experiences, sexual experiences, service to others, the pursuit of science, religious faith, etc.)

The low self-esteem starts with the false belief that we need an excess of the things that we do not have. This continues with the belief that we are those things as we continue losing interests in ourselves and not being grateful for what we have as we focus more and more on the lack. The recovery from low self-esteem starts with taking baby steps by converting "I won't" to "I can't" to "I want" to "How do I" to "I'll try" to "I can" to "I will" to finally achieving "Yes—I did."

The absolute truth remains that it is impossible to be anything other than "self-confident" when we view ourselves from the same angle that our creator does. The distortion from viewing the bases that Maslow had noted above from the view of our EGO creates a mirage of the lack, initiating the search to question our self-esteem and leading to the mirage of less than perfection.

The Paradigm Shift

We all have these images of how we see the world, ourselves, others, everything related to our personal experiences, and our interpretations of them. However, we never see the world as is because we are only capable of seeing the world as how we are. This image of what we have in our head is our paradigm. In order to change how we see ourselves and the world, we must shift our paradigm to what is desired.

This means that the path of bringing change to our experiences requires creation of a paradigm shift. In the path of ease and sometimes from the fear of unknown, we find comfort in our habits as we become more and more habitual beings and do what is more familiar to us. We bond ourselves to these habits even if sometimes they may not be desirable.

Our habits are formed by three prerequisites of knowledge, skill, and desire. We must explore to evaluate and reevaluate each of these criterions in order to change the path of least resistance of our habits to shift our paradigm.

Since change comes when we act above our environment, we must be prepared to experience some level of discomfort as we gain understanding during our new transition to the new comfort level.

One may say that this paradigm shift and transition is a part of our maturity. We mature at a rate starting with our dependency as we move to independency and finally recognize our interdependency.

Interdependency is when we recognize that we are a thread of a specific pattern of this beautiful creation. Any change of this thread will change and impact the pattern of the tapestry of creation as a whole. We recognize that our energetic being requires harmony with all energetic forms, and each individual change leads to a wave, like a droplet of water in a pond that will create waves impacting all beings. In a way, our actions with their energetic substances will echo through eternity as the first law of thermodynamics assures us that energy will not die.

T.S. Eliot said, "We shall not cease from exploration. And the end of all our exploring will be to arrive where we started and know the place for the first time." In this path of inquiry and growth from dependency to interdependency, we will realize that voluntarily or involuntarily paradigm shifts have allowed us to grow, allowing us to have a different view and interpretation of the same events of our lives.

Our biggest paradigm shift is when we finally realize that we must seek to understand before seeking to be understood. When we understand, we become compassionate and resolve to find resolutions. When we do not, we challenge and struggle with all the understandings that we had viewed as misunderstandings before.

We know when our paradigm is in line with universal laws and is ageless when our focus remains on group wellness as a whole, with our desires leading the way with love, joy, and happiness. Under this condition, when our desires are satisfied, the love, joy, and happiness will not be lessened and they will remain eternal, unlike the shifts that occur when the driving force is driven by our needs.

> "You never change things by fighting the existing reality. To change something, build a new model that makes the existing model obsolete." — BUCKMINSTER FULLER

"The Path to Effectiveness"!

Have you ever experienced that sometimes there are a lot of actions and efforts in our transactions without being effective? It seems that a lot of energy and efforts are used but without producing results or having accomplishments.

Effectiveness can apply to all our transactions, be they personal, social, business or political. Our methods to be effective or not have the tendency to become our habits and soon become a part of our personality and how we view and accomplish everything.

We are most effective when the desired result is 100% complete, meeting a certain criteria and utilizing the minimum amount of needed effort as the required input energy.

We become goal oriented and will get the job done and excel in whatever we put our focus on when we are effective. When we are not effective, we may be qualified as being failures, being busy bodies, and being unreliable, since we cannot show results or complete a task impacting our accountability per our promises.

Stephen Covey in his best seller book *The 7 Habits of Highly Effective People* describes the most essential habits of being effective as responsibility, vision, integrity, mutual respect, mutual understanding, creative cooperation, renewals, and continues to the 8th habit as being able to move from effectiveness to greatness.

Since effectiveness can be measured only by each person individually, the question arises, "What is considered to be effective?" A great parent may be very effective in being a parent but this may create ineffectiveness in other areas of his or her life. Or the opposite: being very effective at work and ineffective in personal relationships.

The answer to the above lies in the clarity within us and applying the seven habits internally first before projecting it to the outside world. Clarity comes from understanding what we truly want and being happy with it, since that will be 100% effective regardless of how it may be interpreted by outsiders. If the intention is to have fun going to a game, then wining is no longer important. The effectiveness of having fun is 100% and effectiveness of winning has less value. Wining would be an icing on the cake and its absence will have no impact on the cake as a whole.

However, if going to the game with that intention produces a loss creating unresolved hurt and disappointment then that will show lack of clarity about our intentions due to personal confusion.

Flirting with an idea with no firm determination to get results has a different dynamic than getting it done under all circumstances to be most effective. This does not mean that we should not follow the rule of measuring twice and cutting it once by gathering all the required information before making a decision. Not following through with an idea with 100% ineffectiveness after gathering information supporting lack of good results will be interpreted as total effectiveness due to making the wise choice.

The key to identifying our clarity for the purpose of measuring our effectiveness properly may be the overlap voice that is created by four pillars of our talent, conscious, passion, and need. What we are good at, what we believe is the right thing to do, what we love doing, and what we qualify as being necessary to accomplish what is desired will determine that measuring bar. Our effectiveness can be evaluated under the above criteria producing happiness, joy, and satisfaction regardless of conditions, and with 100% effectiveness.

"Effective people are not problem minded; they're opportunity minded. They feed opportunities and starve problems." — PETER DRUCKER

The Power of Breath

Some cultures define breath as the link that connects our spirit to our physical body at birth, which continues until our last breath when we are separated. Breathing is a very unique part of our physiology which can be changed voluntarily, but if needed, the body will take over automatically.

We breathe about twelve to sixteen times per minute, so we are constantly involved in some form of breathing. The rhythm of our breathing can put us into anxiety or depression, and it can also pull us out of those emotions. The dominate left or right nostril breathing can create mood swings or be used to correct such conditions. In addition, the length of inhale versus exhale can create similar emotional impacts. Breathing can make our body efficient or inefficient, impacting our health and weight.

One of the most important aspects of maintaining an alkaline environment is to have proper oxygen levels, to allow perfect chemical reaction for our system of water being H_2O. When you inhale, each oxygen part that is transferred to your blood stream is picked up via one hemoglobin to be transported to any part of the body cells. When oxygen meets another protein called cytochrome c oxidase, it will make two molecules of water out of every molecule of oxygen. When this happens, there is a little bit of energy released. This energy is needed for the healthy cell's voltage drop of -20 to -25mV in order to have perfect, healthy living conditions and to ensure 7.35 to 7.45 pH alkaline levels.

Food, nutrients, diet, and proper physical activities are very important; however, they are not always consistently used, such as breathing at the rate of nearly 20,000 cycles/day. This is one of the reasons why certain health conditions deteriorate despite the best diets and medical care.

Proper breathing and proper thought management with positive thinking ensures the best possible environment for each cell, which is considered to be our foundation. This constant pinging, like pleasant music, creates a harmonious vibration via the proper voltage across the cells, allowing them to reproduce and be vibrant instead of distressed.

Try these simple breathing points and exercises:

1. Proper breathing is slow, quiet, deep, and regular

2. Inhale through the nose, belly out, and relax the muscles down to the belly

3. Exhale through nose and mouth, belly in, and tighten up the muscles up to top of lungs

4. Avoid shallow mouth and throat breathing, and use the lower part of lungs

5. Follow this optimal cycle: Inhale (2–3 seconds), exhale (3–4 seconds), pause (2–3 seconds)

6. Keep your posture straight and check your breathing often, especially when stressed

7. Exercise #1 (to destress or wake up): Breathe in and out through your nose as fast and long as you can by pushing and pulling your belly out and in (20–60 seconds). Keep your tongue attached to top of your mouth. Follow with eight relaxing breaths

8. Exercise #2: Stand up straight with feet shoulder-width apart. Make fists, holding on to each thumb, and raise them parallel to the floor. Expand your arms out as you breathe in as much as you can, pushing your chest out and raising up on the balls of your feet. Hold for a few seconds and then fall back down with your exhale. It feels as your chest splits open and has more room.

Make a "T" sound at the end of inhale. Do one to three sets with six repetitions each

9. Exercise #3 (for anxiety): Exhale first and then inhale (4 seconds), hold (7 seconds), and exhale (8 seconds). Repeat eight times

So, yawn as much as you need to, listen to your body, keep your spine straight, and breathe regularly when you are stressed, and most important of all, only ponder on good thoughts and let all the other thoughts be gone. Laugh more and worry less, and be comforted in the absolute truth that the default of universe is always good; even when you may not understand its timing, know that it will eventually present itself.

The Power of Expectation

During the 1890s, Ivan Pavlov experimented with dogs by training them to come when a bell rang and then giving them a treat. He measured their saliva each time and showed that they were anticipating food. Eventually the dogs developed a habit and continued to come and salivate in anticipation of food even when the bell was ringing but no food was given to them. This showed that we can develop such realistic habits that our body can anticipate and mobilize toward preparation of an event through an unrelated catalyst, such as a bell that may trigger a physical reaction.

The above is confirmed and is repeated in many of our interactions with others as we grow up. The way others treat us by taking action or by not taking action when we expect them to do so equally sculpts our persona in a way that we no longer act independent from others' behavior. This means that soon there will be enough bells out there that will trigger certain impulses and physical and emotional likes and dislikes in us that they will cause emotional distress without those actual events being present.

This undetected training continues as we start learning to anticipate the outcome of an event based on past history. When this anticipation is positive, we excel, and when this anticipation is negative, we learn to become habitual failures.

In mid-1925, a Copenhagen experiment puzzled why a photon, when shot toward an opening that has two holes, is capable of transforming itself to wave particles in order to show up at the other end as two waves and going through both holes. How could a photon know that there are two holes present instead of just passing through one of the holes? This has been interpreted in different ways, including my personal favorite interpretation and belief that the photon is capable of understanding and tangling its knowledge with the observer. The knowledge of the observer and the degree of their focus determines the outcome as it links all of us vibrationally. This was also further confirmed in more recent experiments similar to the Copenhagen one, where the observer's focus and attention creates higher intensity and probability of this transformation of energy.

With this new understanding, we realize that our anticipation of the outcome will impact the outcome even when we think that no action has been taken to influence that outcome. The power of inaction remains to be a choice that we make internally, determining the outcome ahead of time. In a way, action begins at conception of our intent, when it may not be physically apparent to ourselves and others that any actions have been taken.

So, what can be learned from this new understanding, since we have become accustomed to constantly measuring ourselves based on others' actions or lack of actions?

- When others take no action when you expect them to do so, choose to act independent from their opinions and allow this lack of action to refine you to be more focused toward what you desire, instead of defining you to accept that you may be lacking from your wholeness.

- When you have not yet taken action but it is expected of you, choose to determine the outcome as you desire it before taking action.

The Promise of Future

Future comes exactly as what the promise of future is. The sooner we understand this concept, the sooner we are able to communicate with the universe, which only operates based on that law.

What are the chances of getting a product that we really want by trying to order it from another country when we do not understand their language? How could we possibly communicate to describe the details of what is desired? How could they know where to deliver the product, among many other communication failures, causing unfavorable results?

The universe works exactly the same. Once you communicate with it in the language that it understands and comprehends, all of its unlimited potential will become available to be accessed at will, as it has always intended to be.

Neville Goddard said, in confirmation of what other masters and scriptures had promised to be the technology of creation;

> "You must assume the feeling of the wish fulfilled until your assumption has all the sensory vividness of reality. You must imagine that you are already experiencing what you desire. That is, you must assume the feeling of the fulfillment of your desire until you're possessed by it and this feeling crowds all other ideas out of your consciousness. . . ."

> "So, by assuming the feeling that would be yours were you already in possession of your objective, the subconscious is moved to build the exact likeness of your assumption."

We must recognize that our power remains to be at now, where the promise of peace, joy, and wellness in the future will start. So, if you wonder what your future will be, you must evaluate your current thoughts.

The statistical data on the effect of meditation, when meditating on peace and tranquility versus war and struggle, was finally published in 1987 as the Maharishi Effect. It showed that as more and more people focused on peace, more peaceful events happened around the world, and the rate of crime to humanity decreased during those specific times when at least 1 percent of that population was meditating with having a different focus than others. It showed that a group focus on the promise of what is desired will begin to flourish and becomes reality as it materializes with the change of focus.

We have all experienced getting on a merry-go-round as a child. The merry-go-round requires a certain synchronicity of speed before anyone is able to get on. Any speed faster or slower will bump you off without allowing you to get on to enjoy the ride. In reality, we use the same technology to enjoy riding our desires as the universe provides them. We must synchronize our speed and communication with the universe in order to create a combustion to be able to receive our desires and enjoy them.

> *"You've got to be thrilled at the promise of the future before the promise of future can be yours. You've got to be so excited about your impending wellness that you're not worried about your current illness. It's mood. It's attitude. It's vibration. It's creation."*
> — ESTHER HICKS

"The Quality Of Our Belief!"

We are constantly faced with the question of our belief, since everything that we accomplish is determined by the quality of what we trust that this belief is supposed to be. "Do I truly believe I can do this regardless of what may appear to be?". Only a few really understand the magnitude of its importance and how the outcome will be directed by the quality of this belief.

We all say; "YES we believe we can do it, or NO we believe we cannot". From that moment on, the energetic universe starts preparing the outcome based on that belief. This energetic response is not based on any language using the words YES or NO, since it only replies to the intent and attitude that supports the answer by each individual.

So how does the quality of this belief change the outcome?

Let's say that you ask two people the same question of;

"Do you believe that you can walk from here to another city without stopping?". Each one says; "YES I believe" with absolute certainty. They both start walking and then the storm comes, the rain comes, it gets very cold, there is an earthquake, all the stores are closed and there is no food or water. One of them gets to the other city and the other one does not.

On the way back from that city, the one who made it runs to the other person and asks; what happened? I thought that you believed that you could do it. The other one says; well, the rain and storm came. You respond, "yes I know". But, there was an earthquake and it was cold, and you respond; "yes I know". Finally he/she says, you do not understand, there was no food or water, and you say "yes I know", I am still hungry and thirsty as you are but I have already accomplished what I had believed I could do. So which one really "believed", since both had said that they believed they could do it. What caused only one of them to succeed?

Science now confirms what was given in the scripture as being "the technology for CREATION" through the quality of our belief. It states; "ask without hidden motives" which emphasizes the quality of our belief not having doubts and continues by stating; "surround yourself with your asking so your joyfulness be full".

We create electromagnetically by developing an energetic field of our desires and combining our thoughts through an electric field followed by our emotions which are electrochemical reactions. Neville Goddard said; "assume the feeling as you already have it".

So next time that you are faced with the question of believing if you can do it or not, whether it is internal or raised by others, consider evaluating your answer to assure that your belief matches your vibrational intention by doing the following;

Keep the thought related to the outcome uncontaminated without any doubts by having a single positive thought and focus and keep repeating it as needed.

Visualize and feel having the desired outcome, exactly as if you would have liked, as if you already have it.

The Question of "Good Enough"

I hope that one day there will be a candid camera video of the reactions of all the people who died after struggling with the question of "Am I good enough?" in their living states.

I can imagine what that video would look like. There would be a lot of surprise, sorrow, and regret, with people saying; "I wish I had known this when I was alive" that "I was born good enough, I lived good enough" and "I died being good enough."

At this state of fearless being, I can see that it was impossible for me to be anything other than good enough.

One may inquire about the source of this question and wonder how it ever started. No one really knows what this question means, since it seems to be constantly changing based on how we view things as we grow. Somehow, lack of this gives us the feeling of having a hole in our wholeness, which is interpreted as being less or not being good enough.

If all was good and wholeness was defined by it, then anything less than good must have had some bad in it, to be defined as being less to initiate the question of being good enough. The conversion of this goodness to something less may be summarized in the process of exchanging our energetic fullness of power with a lesser physical strength of force as we become more physically acquainted with our ego-driven body.

Since power is our energetic essence and force is our physical action, we can never find power by learning how to be more forceful. Along this path of confusion, we lose our power and start looking into recovering it by gaining more force. We become less and less powerful, doubting who we truly are and how good we are and whether we are good enough to be or not to be.

Power comes from the authority and energy that has provided it all with grace through each heartbeat. It is given to all of us without prejudice, and it is our essence. No one can take it away unless we are willing to give it away when we get confused and block its freely provided path.

The only way to remove the lens that has created this confusion is by recognizing our true power. Since force is physical and power is energetic, and we are made of 99.9 percent energy, then the answer will be to affirm our energetic essence to regain our wholeness.

When our energy flows freely, we interpret it as being at ease, loving, and joyful, and when it is not flowing with ease, we call it conditional with dis-ease. Then, power comes from loving without conditions, and force comes from anything other than that which is embedded in conditions.

Consequently, the answer may lie in this simple affirmation. Every time the question of being good enough arises, we need to remind ourselves of who we truly are by stating that "I am love, I am loving, and I am beyond that." This will need to continue with affirmative reminders that love is generated from self to self and cannot be found in a source outside, and can only overflow to the outside and others when it has been filled to the rim internally. When the cup is overflowing, there is no space for lack of its wholeness raising the question of being good enough.

If someone treats you badly and initiates the doubt of being good enough, just remember: There is something wrong with them, not you, since it is impossible for you to be anything other than good enough.

The Science Behind Reaching Your Desired Goals

In order for an arrow to hit the bull's eye, it must have the following components:

1. A sharp tip for clarity of direction.

2. A straight and strong stem that will maintain the clarity of the path to the target.

3. The power behind the bow, pulling it to give the arrow the energy to get to the target.

This is how the above translates into accomplishing your goal once it is set:

1. Your thought is like the tip of the arrow, and its clarity will provide the sharpness needed.

2. Your determination is like the stem that ensures the path will maintain its course and travels, regardless of all friction.

3. Your power of emotion is the energy that will fuel all that is needed to ensure you reach your goal.

However, the most important step is to ensure that all desired goals are congruent with the universe's flow of love and peace.

The Silent Voice Within

Studies have shown that something amazing happens in multiple personality disorder patients that defies medical science. In one personality, they may show a fatal allergic reaction to something, but in their other personality, they show no reaction to it at all. In some cases, they have even shown that their eye color changes with the different personalities.

This remarkably conflicts with all that we believe to know about our physical limitations, our health, and miraculous healings opposing the odds provided by science.

This may also be paralleled by the placebo effect. On average, +/-20 percent of medical drug studies have shown that the same results occur within the groups of those who take no drugs but only think they did. So, if the placebo works to bring healing then, nocebo should work too, making us sick by believing.

How can this knowledge be utilized to allow us to learn from this and regain our forgotten power of that silent voice that makes internal suggestions? That inner voice can make us powerful or powerless.

Hypnosis has shown that a person can be hypnotized with brain frequency activity levels near theta, or about 7.5 Hz. This means that the hypnotized person can be directed to pick up an eraser and erase something or be told that the eraser is a hot rock. If the person is told that the same eraser is a hot rock, the subject can barely touch it and his skin will show actual signs of a burn and a rash. Under both conditions the eraser is the same; however, something has shifted internally inside the person's awareness that has impacted his belief.

This means that our physical body can take directions from that silent voice in a specific way that is not available to us when it is generated with mental activity as it ramps up to the beta levels of our daily routines. However, when our active brain is full of positive thoughts, it will keep the beta-level stress at the lowest levels, minimizing the body's stress. At the same time, when this becomes habitual, positive, low-stress thinking, it will train us to operate our body at optimum efficiency, which results in more joyful, more peaceful, and happier personal experiences.

So, it is reassuring to know that meditation and conducive positive thinking will lead to positive being, which allows the brain's frequency ranges to be near low alpha and high theta levels. This may be interpreted that we are all capable of miraculous healing by guiding the physical body when we achieve the level of focus similar to the hypnosis and multilevel personality examples above. In that state, we can direct the body toward instant healing with a single thought of a silent voice within, same as a yogi's state of *Samadhi*, where miracles happen.

Also, the best time to make any kind of habitual transformation or behavior shift is just before we fall asleep or just before we wake up. A short, positive affirmation repeated in a relaxed state during those times will produce amazing results.

"When I am silent, I have thunder hidden inside." — RUMI

The Vibration of a Statue

Entertain yourself for a few minutes and follow these steps. You will be amazed to find out more about yourself:

1. Pick your favorite, most loveable animal

2. Pick your least favorite, most horrific animal

3. Get some clay (real or imaginary) and make a statue of each of the animals (or purchase one)

4. Monitor your emotions as you make each statue

5. Put one on each night stand on either side of your bed

Now, start monitoring yourself for a few days or weeks as you go to bed, when you wake up, or any time that you see these statues.

Most likely you will notice that you feel differently each time you see these statues. When you go to bed or get up from the side where the statue of the animal that scares you is located (as you bring your attention to it), you will feel stressed, you will become angry easily for no reason, you may experience nightmares, and more. Each time that you go to bed or get up from the side where you put the lovable favorite animal, you will maintain neutrality, or you will feel at ease, elevated, comforted, and loving, you will have pleasant dreams, and more.

After a while, your behavior will change and unknowingly you may totally stop going to bed or getting up from the side where your horrific statue is located.

The thoughts leading to your love or hate for that animal will give life to the statue. Like the woodcarver who gave life to Pinocchio, you have given life to this statue, and it lives only in your experience when no one else can recognize nor associate with that feeling except you.

History has shown us that all tyrants and rulers learned to destroy all the monuments and flags of the other party upon victory to disconnect all the emotions with previous representations of such lively appearances. At best, they kept them in museums to be valued as a part of history for those interested in looking for them.

Compassion is when we feel others' pain as our own when we have not experienced it personally. This means that only with compassion can someone else can share a small portion of your pain and fear of looking at the fearful statue, otherwise they view it as just a piece of clay. So, if you walk with a Holocaust victim by a monument made in honor of their torturers, will you feel their pain? Can you convince them that it is just a clay statue preserved for history?

Compassion tells us that it must be eliminated. Wisdom tells us that it should be kept in museums and studied as history, so its horror can be learned from and avoided in the future.

So, what do you see when you look at others in different shapes, colors, clothing, and features, who are made of flesh instead of clay? Question the authority of those feelings when you observe them and how you react to them based on those preconceived emotions.

How often do you give others life in your inside world based on who you think they may be instead of who they truly are? Only with compassion can you remove the lens of fear and truly see others as they are.

"Practice compassion even if no one else does." — LAMA RINPOCHE

The Victim Mentality

Imagine that you buy a calculator and somehow two plus two is programmed to be seven instead of four. You try to balance your checkbook and it is not balancing, which becomes frustrating. Then you go to store and have the same struggle with the cashier, and this continues in every transaction for a few days, then months and years. Soon you start wondering, *Why are all these people against me and cheating me out of something that is rightfully mine?*

A belief is a repetitive thought after thought after thought enforced by experiences. So soon after several experiences, you will believe yourself to be a victim and you stop taking responsibility for your actions. *Why do they do that to me? It is not my fault? Why do bad things always happen to me?* And so on.

Regardless of the possible causes for this misalignment of seven instead of four, how can we realign ourselves, and when would be the right time to do it?

The right time presents itself when we no longer tolerate the dis-ease that this attitude has caused us.

The desire to be more joyful overcomes the discomfort of excuses. The joy of being a deliberate creator substitutes the fallacy of the belief that you are stuck in the world of creation by default.

You are empowered by the truth that you have the power to choose differently rather than believing that what you are experiencing which will move you forward.

Allowing yourself to forgive and let go regardless of the conditions will be all the fuel needed for your new journey toward a joyful destination.

Success is imminent when the attitude shifts from "What can I personally get or achieve?" to "What can I contribute to impact all for the better?"

When they asked the Dalai Lama who had been his greatest teacher, he named the Chinese general who ordered the destruction of his temple and was responsible for his exile.

Time

We have all experienced traveling to different places as time changes. It moves a few hours ahead or behind. Even in some part of the world it may be totally opposite. However, wherever we go and regardless of how we may define time, the measure of an hour still remains the same. The place where it is 2:00 a.m. rather than 2:00 p.m. still accounts for one hour, same as the other place.

Of course, science tells us that if we put a clock inside a train and speed up the train, the clock lags behind to the point that at speed of light, the clock stops, and time vanishes.

So why is it that when we are stressed, it seems like we always have much less time, like we are out of time and our patience relevant to time is much shorter? On the contrary, when we are joyful and happy and loving, it seems like we forget about time as if it does not exist, and it appears that we have more time than in stressful occasions.

When we are fearful and anxious about our future, time goes much faster. When we are joyful, happy, and living in the now, time stops. When we are in a state of sorrow and live in the past, it appears that time moves more slowly, as if it is stuck.

So, if the hour is still the same hour, then how could this be possible? The answer lies with the interpreter, or each of us, as the observer of what we know as "time" and our perception of it.

Many people with near-death experiences report that our perception of time is not correct. We believe that time moves, and we have to wait for it to pass, and believing in it will be the determining factor of what will happen next. However, they report that this is the living's misconception and is not true. Time is constant, and we move through it with our actions.

This means that when we speed up, time appears to move faster, and when we slow down, time appears to move slower.

The above supports how the universe views our actions and what its default is intended to be. If time does not exist, then the universe's intention would be for us to behave in a way where we do not perceive time as faster or slower, and only as that which does not exist. The only time that we behave in a certain way and have that interpretation of time is when we act lovingly, with acceptance and joy, when time appears to be nonexistent.

———"Time" old friend is passing by again

When I was young, I prayed for you to be faster

So I could grow up to be the best that I can be

So I could explore to taste what I had once thought to be impossible

So I could change the world for better than when I had come

So I could find Joy in all that I can touch

But you deceived me my old friend, for in joy there may be sorrow,

as you ought to let go of all you borrow

The Children whom we knew have children

The elders whom we knew are no more

The beautiful clay pot that I loved is chipped

All is changed but you remain the same, steadfast in your descent

Your signature has left nothing but an end

An end that's yet to start with fleeting delay

I cherish each moment in your bosom, knowing that my flower is ready to blossom.

(Dedicated to Dad, February 15, 2009)

"To Look Forward"!

Milarepa, one of the most powerful yogis of Tibet was sent by his sadhu to another master to learn more about what he wanted to accomplish. When he reached his master's cave and approached him from behind, his master said, "Come forward and face me, since I have vowed not to look back."

Can you imagine the power, strength, and confidence that allows one to gather all the wisdom and wanting to look only forward without any desire or willingness to look back? Can you imagine the joy, peace, and love that accumulate all the wisdom by learning from the lessons and moving forward when leaving all the baggage and negative experiences behind?

Many of us become prisoners of our past experiences, not realizing that those were only single experiences and not life sentences. They say that the average person has about 64,000 thoughts per day, but most of them are the same ones they had yesterday.

Milarepa was imprisoned by the thoughts of his past and was not able to move forward to learn more about what he wanted to accomplish. His master guided him to move from that state by giving him the following advice:

"The mind has no leash, thoughts become strong and reckless, and visions emerge from chaos, if you are trapped by these illusions, you will accomplish nothing!"

How do we gain the strength and awareness to recognize that we are entrapped in the web of our past and have bonded with an illusion that no longer exists but continues to haunt us? Our nature is to bond, attach, and develop a kinship to what we are surrounded with that matches our vibrational frequency. Our power and strength come from the ability to choose. The choice is simple and stems from our personal decision to align ourselves with that energy that beats our hearts or not.

Since the energy that beats our hearts only promotes goodness, love, and joy, regardless of any religion, faith, social status, or physical criteria, it always remains to be the absolute base. When we choose to align ourselves only with that energy, we have no tolerance for anything else, including all past experiences that may promote different outcomes. This alignment gives us the strength to not bond to what is not desired. It allows us to let go of the history that is no longer serving us.

When our alignment shifts from that universal base to something different promoted by others' misalignments, we become unsecure, fearful, and in our fear of not being able to find a replacement, we bond ourselves to negative experiences and soon fall into being habitual negative thinkers.

Self-confidence and independent thinking promote us to stop dancing to the empty drummers of the past and others and move forward by tuning ourselves to the music of the universe generated by the energy that beats all hearts.

Portia Nelson said:

"I walk down the street. There is a deep hole in the sidewalk. I fall in. I am lost . . . I am helpless. It isn't my fault. It takes forever to find a way out.

I walk down the same street. There is a deep hole in the sidewalk. I pretend I don't see it. I fall in again. I can't believe I am in the same place. But it isn't my fault. It still takes me a long time to get out.

I walk down the same street. There is a deep hole in the sidewalk. I see it is there. I still fall in. It's a habit. My eyes are open. I know where I am. It is my fault. I get out immediately.

I walk down the same street. There is a deep hole in the sidewalk. I walk around it.

I walk down another street."

War or a Cup of Tea?

My son was sitting reading his children's book next to me one day as I was writing. He quietly said, "Dad, war is sad. You should write about it." I said, "I agree. What should we call it?" He said, "War or a cup of tea."

Since I truly believe that children are our true teachers, I immediately became quiet to tap into his unpolluted wisdom. He continued about the book that he was reading, which was about a village where some of the natives were turning into werewolves, and the rest of the villagers were preparing themselves for a war with their old friends.

At the same time, other villagers were looking for solutions to bring peace to the village and were aggressively focused on having peace. Although some of the villagers had turned into werewolves physically, the other villagers who sought war had become even worse with their attitudes. The villagers who were looking for peace finally succeeded in finding an herb that, when consumed as tea, turned the werewolves back to humans, and the angry people who were seeking war became nice again.

So, a cup of tea avoided war. What a great concept!

Well, this cup of tea is available to all of us; all we need to do is to look for it inside, like the pearl that is hidden inside the shell. Close your eyes and point to yourself. Over the years that I have posed this question to different people, I have never seen anyone point to any part of themselves but their heart. This is simply because we energetically know the tea is hidden inside our heart.

The fourth heart chakra energy, with its green color and its function to only love, is the herb that makes the tea with love and compassion, and guides us to look for all other options other than war. Compassion is when the left and right brain come together to stop all judgment, as we feel the pain of others as ourselves. This allows the heart's energy to radiate out as intended by the universe, without obstruction of our brain-made ego. One may ask, "How could you possibly hurt others if you feel their pain as your own?"

Studies done by Heart-Math Institute as well as others have shown that heart frequencies are several times stronger than our brain. They placed a boy and his dog in two separate rooms and monitored their heartbeats. They each had different heartbeats. They brought the dog to the boy's room, and as soon as the two of them saw each other, their heart frequencies harmonized and synced to the same peak and valleys, like beating as one. It's amazing that love heals all wars and, when the focus is on peace, there is no room left for entertaining anything else.

Lao Tzu said, "The slaying of multitudes should be mourned with sorrow. A victory should be celebrated with the funeral rite." There is no victory in oppression of others, regardless of who is succeeding, since all post-traumatic war studies have shown that all are wounded when exposed to the horror of war, regardless of what happened to their bodies and which side they represented. Historically, most wars have been in the name of maintaining peace and order against aggressors, but jumping out of a plane and thinking afterward about a missing parachute may be too late for action. Peace must arise with every step we take and cannot be a destination.

What Happens When 2+2=7?

It appears that there is a universal understanding among people, students, teachers, businesses, accountants, and nations that two plus two is equal to four. This means that when you go to the store, look for your desired item, inquire about its cost, and the clerk says four dollars, you pay four dollars. You will be expediently and courteously greeted and handed the purchased item to enjoy. This happens many times over as you go to the bank, buy and sell things, and perform many similar transactions.

Now let's assume that for whatever reason you believe that two plus two equals seven. You go to the same clerk and ask for the same item for four dollars. However, you will soon find yourself escorted out of the store without any product, since making a mutual transaction did not happen. All your other transactions with others will lead to exhaustion, disappointment, frustration, and much unfinished businesses as you remain confused about why you cannot get results.

The above is a simple example of how all our relationships are structured internally with ourselves and externally with others. We are born with a clear universal understanding that two plus two equals four, and somehow that gets distorted as we age, leading to unhappiness, struggle, and friction that causes stress, diseases, and more.

Where did we get this universal understanding of four that once we have it and utilize it, everything is created rapidly, joyfully, and receptively, with positive results? How did we ever replace it with a misunderstanding of seven, which makes us struggle in everything we do with disappointment? We energetically communicate with the universe. When we are clear in our asking and expect to receive what is desired, the energetic communication is clear and fruitful. When this communication is distorted, the universe's response is confused and is unsuccessful, since it cannot understand seven when it comprehends four.

The combustion of creation requires a clarity of vibrational intention. Per Esther Hicks (from her book; "The Laws of Attraction"), this can be summarized with three universal laws: the Law of Attraction, the Law of Deliberate Creation, and the Law of Allowing.

> "Ask without hidden motive and be surrounded by your
> answer. Be enveloped by what you desire, that your gladness
> be full." — ORIGINAL ARAMAIC PRAYER

Physicists have discovered that when we give attention to something, we are creating, whether we know it or not. Once this attention is combined with emotion, the combustion of creation will occur. In two plus two equals four, we create via our clear attention and positive emotions, and in two plus two equals seven, we make noise and wonder why we cannot create.

The foundation of this question may be summarized as the confusion stemming from our relationship with the infinite and how we value ourselves, and that in searching for more in the name of ego, we lose our essence of being joyful with less.

Carl Jung said:

> "The decisive question for man is: Is he related to something infinite or not? That is the telling question of his life. Only if we know that the thing which truly matters is the infinite can we avoid fixing our interests upon futilities, and upon all kinds of goals which are not of real importance. Thus, we demand that the world grant us recognition for qualities which we regard as personal possessions: our talent or our beauty. The more a man lays stress on false possessions, and the less sensitivity he has for what is essential, the less satisfying is his life. He feels limited because he has limited aims, and the result is envy and jealousy. If we understand and feel that here in this life we already have a link with the infinite, desires and attitudes change."

What If You Are Having a Bad Day?

Have you ever had a day where everything seems to be going wrong? Or, have you ever been around someone who may be experiencing that, and it seems that no matter what your answer to their question is, it's always the wrong answer?

How could everything be wrong that day? The simple question to ask would be, "What is it that you really want, and is there anything that would be pleasing to you?"

You will immediately find out that there is no right answer that will be pleasing to you and that no amount of right answers from others will satisfy your need not to be irritated. The reason is simple. You are not looking for happiness and joy that day; you want to be miserable and irritated, and we always find what we are looking for.

The people who look for reasons to be offended are rarely disappointed; the people who look for love always find it; the people who look for fights will definitely get into a fight; and the ones who want to be at peace will have a peaceful day.

When you are in love, the world seems loving. You greet the mailman with open arms and ask about his kids. When you have a reason to hate something, the mailman is delivering the same mail and you are so frustrated that he has never delivered the mail the way you like it, when in reality nothing has changed other than your view of the world.

> *"The most important decision we make is whether we believe we live in a friendly or hostile universe."* — ALBERT EINSTEIN

Some studies have shown that motors and electromagnetic fields, such as in equipment and computers, tend to fail more often when the operators do not have positive energy and are in a bad mood. This means that when you feel negative, more negative events will magnetically find their way into your experience that day.

What could be causing this? Lack of proper sleep, physical discomfort, reading or watching disturbing movies or books before going to bed, going to bed with disturbing thoughts, worrying about upcoming events, being overwhelmed and overcommitted with responsibilities—of course everything starts with a thought and more.

What could be the energetic reason for this? Peace only resides at NOW. When we direct our focus to the past or worry about the future, we set ourselves up to mourn the past or feel anxiety about the future. That means we have more potential to promote negativity when we are physically but not mentally present at now.

What can we do if we ever experience this? The first step to recovery is to simply remain at present at NOW, where peace is, and to stop all thoughts about the past or future. Allow yourself to simply and humbly be irritated, to allow what has been stored inside you to pass through. This emotion is foreign to your being and it cannot reside within you, so it will leave you as soon as you allow it. Put up no resistance, no confrontation within yourself to suppress what you are experiencing. Simply repeat to yourself that it is OK that you are irritated, and you are going to experience that irritation, and ask yourself why you are irritated without trying to justify all the reasons that you should not be. Acknowledge the reasons for your irritation and simply remain irritated until the feeling is gone.

Why Do We Experience Dis-ease?

If you decide to wiggle your finger and wonder how you did that, there are many scientifically accurate machines and doctors who are able to scan your brain and your body and show you the exact moment that you made that decision and what happened physically after that.

However, that is not the only decision that you made. There was a decision before that, when you decided to decide, where no one has been able to explain where it comes from.

The decision to decide comes from the driver behind the machine that is not your brain yet guides you in many ways. It is the part of you that can never be physical, and yet it maintains its connection energetically. It is a part of you that cannot relate to any energy with frequencies lower than love, joy, peace, and compassion.

Your interpretation of your life experiences is broken down into two parts: ease and dis-ease. When your energy and action are aligned with the driver behind the scenes, your experience is being at optimum ease. When your energy and action are not aligned with the driver behind the scenes, this is electrically qualified as additional stress to reduce the energy flowing through your body, or dis-ease.

Your first response to this dis-ease may go consciously undetected by you as it develops into emotional dis-ease and continues further to physical dis-ease, which we commonly qualify as disease or sickness.

Let all your decisions be congruent with universal flow of love, joy, peace, and compassion.

Will Your Nose Grow If You Lie?

Most of us are familiar with the fictional story of Pinocchio, where the wishes of an old woodcarver are granted by a fairy, and life is given to the little wooden boy named Pinocchio. The wooden boy soon learned that his new body reacted in a certain way when he was deceitful: his nose grew larger each time he lied.

One may say this would be a very good feature to have, in order to keep everyone honest. All airport security, lawsuits, disputes among people, criminal activity, and suspicions among nations would be eliminated if we had a feature where when we lied or were dishonest, our nose grew. What an amazing concept!

So why don't we have such a feature, if our creator is so perfect and our body is such a perfect creation that all its architecture has been impeccably planned? Well, the answer is simple! You cannot give away what you do not have. You cannot plan for something that you can never anticipate existing. If your understanding is that it is impossible to lie and be dishonest, then there is no need for planning to deal with it in the first place. The source has no concept nor understanding of such behavior.

In order to lie, you must experience fear first. In order to be fearful, you must have something missing from your true essence of unconditional love that's causing you to have conditions imposed by fear. In order to detect fear, you must recognize that there is a threat. In order to acknowledge a threat, you must realize that there is something to protect. Accordingly, in order to understand lying and dishonesty, you will need to investigate its roots for what is being protected.

So, the answer to the question raised initially is yes, your body registers something different when you lie and when you are being dishonest, but not like Pinocchio. However, it is not as if it was planned anticipating that we may lie, it is more as if it is interrupting the flow of universal energy by going the opposite direction. Very much like a car going against one-way traffic.

As was mentioned before; nonverbal communication studies have shown that our body gestures, blinking, and eye positions change when we lie. This is proven to have some credibility, although at times it may be hard to detect and can be subject to the expert's interpretations. A polygraph machine or lie detector is designed to look for physiological changes when we are dishonest. Research has shown that lying increases heartrates, blood pressure, and sweat rates; it causes panting; and our muscles become weaker. These are signs of body experiencing stress.

Basically, we are designed to go downstream, like rafting down a river, when we are loving, joyful, honest, and compassionate, since it is the universe's natural flow of energy. We go upstream when we lie and are dishonest, exposing ourselves to extra stress, friction, inefficiency, and drain on our energetic resources. This reduces our immune system and results in sadness and anger, and it will make us more susceptible to physical and emotional diseases, which in a way will be much more harmful than just having our nose grow like Pinocchio.

So, the question would be this: Do you want your nose to grow or your immune system to drop? The answer is neither; just be honest and truthful, and enjoy the downstream ride of the universal flow.

Your Attitude: Win-Lose, Win-Win, Lose-Win, Lose-Lose

We energetically interact with others with our belief and our vibrational intention before any verbal or nonverbal communication occurs. Language is a very poor translator, since it is subject to many internal interpretations.

Our relationship with ourselves and others has a certain vibrational frequency, same as musical notes. Some pieces of music are pleasant, and some are considered noise by listeners.

The outcome of interactions between any two vibrational beings, internally with themselves and then externally with others, always pivots on the end result of creating music or noise as this blending of frequencies occurs.

The harmonics of two frequencies create a new one. Like oil and water, these frequencies either clash and become noise or they attract each other and harmonize as pleasing music.

Regardless of all variables forming our intention, we usually find ourselves with an attitude that falls into one of these four main categories; win-lose, win-win, lose-win, or lose-lose. This will energetically determine the outcome of our interaction with ourselves and then with others.

Win-lose: "I have no problem with you as long as you do what I want you to do." Lack of respect for themselves and others, covering it with a large ego and manipulation of others. Children who were brought up with conditional love, who don't find value in themselves, and who feel valuable only when they earn something tangible or gain some special status. Full of dirty tricks. Never satisfied and wanting more. Always needing to use force, authority, and manipulation in order to be satisfied and to interact.

Lose-win: "I always lose so you might as well win." Have low self-worth. Great prey for win-lose attitudes at first, until they realize that the abuse is not conducive to their well-being and the universal default of their greatness will eventually erupt, which forces them to seek equilibrium.

Lose-lose: "If I lose, I will take everyone down with me." When two win-lose attitudes meet, eventually one will lose, and lose-lose attitudes will begin to create a lose-lose outcome for both parties. Also, it may promote attitudes that are detached from everyone else: "If I cannot win, then everyone has to lose because if they lose more than I do, I may feel better."

Win-win: The win-win attitude encompasses a compassionate caring and loving attitude that becomes apparent to others, representing respect for all and creating a different energetic flow. It shows integrity, recognition of the fact that self-value is not established in external sources, that commitments are important unless mutually revised, that the view of universe is that all is well and available for everyone, and that one's success will not diminish the other's resources in the abundant universe. It comes from a knowing to reach for all that is desired with compassion for ourselves and others together as whole.

There is an absolute attitude that may be considered the universal attitude that surpasses all. This is simply the WIN attitude! It considers that the glass is always full, the sun always shines, the rain is our connection to heaven, love always flows, compassion never diminishes, fear has no hostage, respect is the only language, and joy is always welcome.

You know you have a WIN attitude when you wake up in the morning and dance to the sound of music while no one is playing.

Your Valentine

Hafiz said, "Even after all this time, the sun never says to the Earth, 'You owe me.' Look what happens with a love like that. It lights the whole sky."

There are several different stories about Saint Valentine's origin and controversies around the events of his life. He was a Roman priest persecuted in the third century who performed weddings for outcasts who were forbidden to marry by the church. The Roman Empire had experienced that young unmarried men were better soldiers than the ones who had emotional ties through marriage, and therefore some of them were forbidden to get married. Saint Valentine performed ceremonies for those soldiers and ministered to the Christians who were persecuted under the Roman Empire.

Legend says that he performed miracles with unconditional love and even healed the blindness of the daughter of the judge who sent him to prison. On February 14, the morning of his persecution, he wrote a letter signed "Your Valentine" as a farewell to his jailer's daughter, whom he had healed.

He was commemorated, martyred, and buried at a cemetery on the Via Flaminia, near Rome.

Writing a letter showing our love for humanity and for the family member of one persecuting us is incomprehensible for many. But those who align themselves with the force that beats their hearts and who are not distracted by the noise of the empty drummers of others, dare to live it and change history by setting an example for billions to follow.

Swami Ramdas said, "He had gone to India to prove them wrong, but when he saw his guru he could not leave." He said, "Have you ever looked into someone's eyes who is looking back at you with complete unconditional love?"

It is a universal magnet that will penetrate your heart. It does so simply because it is our essence; it is what is inside, and when it finds itself, it melts your heart in bliss, reminding you that you are home again as if you had never left.

Is there a sound of wind in the forest if there is no ear to hear it? For whatever reason, the ear that captures that resonance enjoys the sound of the forest as pleasing music. In a way, the reflection of a romantic love or a platonic love between two people who recognize the connectivity of their souls resonates the same and even amplifies that love beyond ecstasy. What better way to celebrate this recognition than on the day that a master was persecuted for that message, so he knows that his message in the forest was heard at last.

(Dedicated to my wife, Tammy)

AFTERWARD

The end . . . or . . . the beginning to hear your voice within?

This book has no conclusion, since the intention to have a conclusion is affirming a closure for an ending. This book is about a new beginning for no one else but you to truly see the "eye of an I."

This book is about offering what John Newton experienced when as a slave trader in the 18th century was enlightened to become an abolitionist to write the song Amazing Grace:

"I once was lost but now I am found. Was blind, but now I see."

This book is about the six blind men who ran into an elephant and tried to figure out what it was. One touches the leg and says that it must be a tree. One touches the body and says that it is a wall. One touches the tail and says that it must be a rope. One touches the ears and says that they are floppy so it must be a bird. One touches the trunk and says that it must be a snake, and the last one touches the tusks and says it must be a spear. Although each of them had a point of view, none of them saw the elephant as it truly was.

If you started the beginning of this book as one of the blind men, the hope is that by the end you recognize that it is only by aligning yourself with that voice within that guides you at all times and beats your heart, and all hearts, that you can truly see the elephant—as beautiful and majestic as it truly is.

Only then you can recognize your true magnificence,

and indeed, it is an amazing grace!